UNWIN HYMAN COLLECTIONS

SOLID GROUND

INCLUDING FOLLOW ON ACTIVITIES

EDITED BY JANE LEGGETT AND SUE LIBOVITCH

Unwin Hyman English Series

Series editor: Roy Blatchford
Advisers: Jane Leggett and Gervase Phinn

Unwin Hyman Short Stories

Unwin Hyman Collections

Unwin Hyman Plays

Published in 1988 by
Unwin Hyman Limited
15–17 Broadwick Street
London W1V 1FP

British Library Cataloguing in Publication Data

Solid Ground. — (Unwin Hyman collections).
1. Women. Rights – Serials
I. Leggett, Jane   II. Libovitch, Sue
323.3'4

ISBN 0-7135-2842-7

Typeset in Great Britain by TJB Photosetting Ltd., South Witham, Lincolnshire
Printed in Great Britain by Billing & Sons Ltd., Worcester
Series cover design by Iain Lanyon
Cover illustration by Anne Magill

Contents

INTRODUCTION

'Solid Ground' is a collection of writing by women, and spans a century of their experience.

The collection falls broadly into two catagories: extracts from autobiographical writing which speak directly of particular experiences, and short stories which offer a more general picture of women's experience. The pieces are drawn from different countries and reflect a variety of social and cultural traditions.

The central themes of the collection focus on resistence rather than repression and on re-defining rather than acquiescing. While each piece can stand on its own, it is hoped that collectively they will encourage further reading to discover more about an issue, country, time in history, or the work of a particular writer.

Women have always been storytellers, passing on experience, knowledge and imagination from one generation to another, but until the recent past only a few have gained widespread recognition for their ideas. The discovery and re-discovery of writing by women has led to an explosion of publications which we can now enjoy and share with our students. As English teachers, we have had some success in integrating work around issues of gender and anti-sexism into the curriculum we offer, not only in girls' schools but in boys' and mixed schools as well. The groundwork done with the younger pupils can now be extended, developed and credited through many English and English Literature examination syllabuses.

The 'Follow On' activities are designed to present a range of writing, talking, and research assignments which will help students to gain in confidence and competence at using and responding to language in a variety of contexts. They have been devised bearing in mind the National Criteria underpinning GCSE English examination courses and aim to assist students in building up a folder of written and oral coursework. Prefacing each suggested assignment is a short introduction which gives some background information about the writer and which helps to place the piece in context. It is important that this is read, and if necessary discussed, before reading. Equally, students are often invited to extend their knowledge and understanding of a particular writer or situation by refering to the titles in 'Further Reading'. Again, teachers may wish to preview some of these titles before reading a story or extract with a group.

Jane Leggett
Sue Libovitch

ANNE PETRY

*T*he Moses of Her People

In 1826 when Harriet Ross was about six years old, she had unconsciously absorbed many kinds of knowledge, almost with the air she breathed. She could not, for example, have said how or at what moment she learned that she was a slave.

She knew that her brothers and sisters, her father and mother, and all the other people who lived in the quarter, men, women and children, were slaves.

She had been taught to say, "Yes, Missus," "No, Missus" to white women, "Yes, Mas'r," "No, Mas'r" to white men. Or "Yes, sah," "No, sah."

At the same time, someone had taught her where to look for the North Star, the star that stayed constant, not rising in the east and setting in the west as the other stars appeared to do; and told her that anyone walking toward the North could use that star as a guide.

She knew about fear, too. Sometimes at night, or during the day, she heard the furious galloping of horses, not just one horse, several horses, thud of the hoofbeats along the road, jingle of harness. She saw the grown folks freeze into stillness, not moving, scarcely breathing, while they listened. She could not remember who first told her that those furious hoofbeats meant the patrollers were going past, in pursuit of a runaway. Only the slaves said patterollers, whispering the word.

She was aware of all these things and many other things too.

She learned to separate the days of the week. Sunday was a special day. There was no work in the fields. The slaves cooked in the quarter and washed their clothes and sang and told stories.

There was another special day, issue day, which occurred at the end of the month. It was the day that food and clothes were issued to the slaves. One of the slaves was sent to the Big House, with a wagon, to bring back the monthly allowance of food. Each slave received eight pounds of pickled pork or its equivalent in fish, one bushel of Indian meal (corn meal), one pint of salt.

Once a year, on issue day, they received clothing. The men were given two tow-linen shirts, two pairs of trousers, one of tow-linen, the other woolen, and a woolen jacket for winter. The grown-ups received one pair of yarn stockings and a pair of shoes.

The children under eight had neither shoes, stockings, jacket nor trousers. They were issued two tow-linen shirts a year—short, one-piece garments made of a coarse material like burlap, reaching to the knees. These shirts were worn night and day. They were changed once a week. When they were worn out, the children went naked until the next allowance day.

And so at six, Harriet already knew fear and uneasiness. She knew certain joys too, the joy of singing, the warmth from a pine-knot fire in a fire-place, the flickering light that served as decoration, making shadows on the walls, changing, moving, dancing, concealing the lack of furniture.

She was accustomed to the scratchy feel of the tow-linen shirt she wore. Because she went bare-footed, the soles of her feet were calloused, but the toes were straight, never having known the pinch of new shoes or any kind of foot covering.

She was a solemn-eyed, shy little girl, slow of speech, but quick to laugh. She was always singing or humming, under her breath, pausing in her play to look upward, watching the sudden free flight of the birds, listening to the cherokee of the redwing blackbirds, watching a squirrel run up the trunk of a tree, in the nearby woods, studying the slow drift of cumulus clouds across a summer sky.

This period of carefree idleness was due to end soon. The

fierce old woman who looked after the children kept telling Harriet that things would change.

Whenever she saw the little girl stop to look at the trees, the sky, she repeated the same harsh-voiced warning. 'Overseer'll be settin' you a task any day now. Then you won't be standin' around with your mouth hangin' open, lookin' at nothin' all day long. Overseer'll keep you movin'.'

In 1831, when Harriet regarded herself sufficiently grown up to wear a bandanna, she kept hearing a strange, fascinating story, told and retold in the quarter, in the fields. This same story about a slave named Tice Davids was being told in the Big House, too. But with a difference. The slaves told it with relish, the masters with distaste. Tice Davids ran away from his master in Kentucky. He planned to cross the Ohio River at Ripley. But his master followed so close behind him that Tice had to jump in the river and swim across.

The master hunted for a boat, and while hunting, never lost sight of Tice, kept watching his head, just above the water, as he swam toward the opposite shore. Once in the boat, the master followed him, saw him plainly, swimming faster and faster. The master drew so near to him that when Tice stood up in the water and started to run, he could see the water splashing about his thighs. He saw him reach the shore. The master grounded the boat, jumped out—not more than five minutes behind the slave.

He never saw Tice Davids again.

The master went back to Kentucky and told about this strange disappearance, how his slave, Tice, had literally vanished before his eyes. Puzzled, disturbed more than he cared to admit, he explained his mystery by saying, 'He must have gone on a underground road.'

Harriet was puzzled by this story. She kept thinking about it. Was there a road that ran under the ground? Was that how Tice Davids had escaped from his master? If Tice could find it, could other people find it, too?

People in the border states, who had been sheltering runaway slaves, helped further the mystery of an underground road. The new steam trains were being talked about everywhere. A rumour started, and spread, to the effect that there was an underground railroad too.

The free Negroes, the Quakers, the Methodists, the German farmers, who helped runaway slaves in Ohio, Pennsylvania, New York, started using phrases and words suited to the idea of a railroad. They called themselves conductors, stationmasters, brakemen. Their houses and barns and haystacks, and the unsuspected secret passages inside the big farmhouses, were called depots and stations. They referred to the runaways' as passengers, parcels, boxes, bales of black wool. Large parcels were grownups; small parcels were children.

In 1831 there were many people like the young Harriet, who believed that there really was a steam train that ran through a deep underground tunnel from South to North, and that a slave who could board it in the South, at some unknown point, would emerge a free man, in a free state, when the train came up out of the ground, snorting and puffing, leaving a trail of smoke and cinders behind it. Certainly the story of Tice Davids suggested this was true.

This mysterious underground railroad was spoken of, in whispers, in the quarter on the Brodas plantation, just as it was on all the other plantations.

In that same year, in August, in October, in November, the slaves in the quarter and the masters in the Big Houses, began to talk about another story. In the quarter, the name of the man who was involved was never spoken aloud. It was always whispered, as though the land, the trees, the sky, the rivers and coves had ears. Its details were known all over the United States. Like the other slaves, Harriet knew the story as accurately and as completely as though she had been an eyewitness to the event.

It was the story of Nat Turner. He was a slave, in Southampton, Virginia. He was called The Prophet. He was a preacher.

When he was a boy, growing up, his mother told him, over and over, that he would be like Moses. He would lead his people out of slavery as Moses had led the children of Israel out of bondage in Egypt. She taught him verses and whole chapters of the Bible which she had memorised. He memorised them too, especially the ones that dealt with the prophets in the Old Testament.

He was a silent, brooding man, given to fasts and contemplation, going often, alone, into the caves of the mountains, in the section of Virginia where he lived. He believed himself to be a prophet. He claimed that he saw visions.

On the night of August 20, 1831, he said to six of his followers: 'Our race is to be delivered from bondage, and God has appointed us as the men to do His bidding; I am told to slay all the whites we encounter, men, women and children ...it is necessary that in the commencement of this revolution all the whites we meet must die'.

They set out together, Nat Turner and his six followers, and at every plantation where they stopped, other slaves joined them, until there were seventy of them altogether. They killed sixty white persons, men, women and children, found on plantations within a radius of twenty miles.

The local militia and Federal troops were called in to quell this unplanned and unrehearsed insurrection. All through the South, slavesholders were terrified. Though one hundred Negroes were killed in the process of putting down this revolt, Nat Turner could not be found. He stayed hidden in a cave in Southampton County for two months. He was finally found, and executed on November 11, 1831.

Also in 1831 Harriet received a blow on the head that was to scar her for the rest of her life. When the overseer had caught a runaway slave, she had refused to help tie him up so that he could be whipped.

In 1844 Harriet married John Tubman, a free man. Then in 1849 she learnt that she was to be sold to work on the chain gang. She tried to persuade John Tubman to escape with her but he refused and even threatened to give her away.

That night when John Tubman was asleep, and the fire had died down in the cabin, she took the hashcake that had been baked for their breakfast, and a good-sized piece of salt herring, and tied them together in an old bandanna. By hoarding this small stock of food, she could make it last a long time, and with the berries and edible roots she could find in the woods, she wouldn't starve.

She decided that she would take the quilt she had lovingly

created for her wedding. Her hand lingered over it. It felt soft and warm to her touch. Even in the dark, she thought she could tell one colour from another, because she knew its pattern and design so well.

Then John stirred in his sleep, and she left the cabin quickly, carrying the quilt carefully folded under her arm. She never saw him again and even though she learnt of his infidelity a few years later, she was deeply saddened by his death in 1867.

Once she was off the plantation, she took to the woods, not following the North Star, not even looking for it, going instead toward Bucktown. She needed help. She was going to ask a white woman who had stopped to talk to her so often if she would help her. Perhaps she wouldn't. But she would soon find out.

When she came to the farmhouse where the woman lived, she approached it cautiously, circling around it. It was so quiet. There was no sound at all, not even a dog barking, or the sound of voices. Nothing.

She tapped on the door gently. A voice said, 'Who's there?' She answered, 'Harriet, from Dr. Thompson's place.'

When the woman opened the door she did not seem at all surprised to see her. She glanced at the little bundle that Harriet was carrying, at the quilt, and invited her in. Then she sat down at the kitchen table, and wrote two names on a slip of paper, and handed the paper to Harriet.

She said that those were the next places where it was safe for Harriet to stop. The first place was a farm where there was a gate with big white posts and round knobs on top of them. The people there would feed her, and when they thought it was safe for her to go on, they would tell her how to get to the next house, or take her there. For these were the first two stops on the underground Railroad – going North, from the Eastern Shore of Maryland.

Thus Harriet learned that the Underground Railroad that ran straight to the North was not a railroad at all. Neither did it run underground. It was composed of a loosely organised group of people who offered food and shelter, or a place of concealment, to fugitives who had set out on a long road to the North and freedom.

Harriet wanted to pay this woman who had befriended her. But she had no money. She gave her the patchwork quilt, the only beautiful object she had ever owned.

That night she made her way through the woods, crouching in the underbush whenever she heard the sound of horses' hoofs, staying there until the riders passed. Each time she wondered if they were already hunting for her. It would be so easy to describe her, the deep scar on her forehead like a dent, the old scars on the back of her neck, the husky speaking voice, the lack of height, scarcely five feet tall. The master would say she was wearing rough clothes when she ran away, that she had a bandanna on her head, that she was muscular and strong.

In the morning, she came to the house where her friend had said she was to stop. She showed the slip of paper that she carried to the woman who answered her knock on the door of the farmhouse. The woman fed her, and then handed her a broom and told her to sweep the yard.

Harriet hesitated, suddenly suspicious. Then she decided that with a broom in her hand, working in the yard, she would look like she belonged on the place, certainly no one would suspect that she was a runaway.

That night the woman's husband, a farmer, loaded a wagon with produce. Harriet climbed in. He threw some blankets over her, and the wagon started.

It was dark under the blankets, and not exactly comfortable. But Harriet decided that riding was better than walking. She was surprised at her own lack of fear, wondered how it was that she so readily trusted these strangers who might betray her. For all she knew, the man driving the wagon might be taking her straight back to the master.

When she finally arrived in Pennsylvania, she had travelled roughly ninety miles from Dorchester County. She had slept on the ground outdoors at night. She had been rowed for miles up the Choptank River by a man she had never seen before. She had been concealed in a haycock, and had, at one point, spent a week hidden in a potato hole in a cabin which belonged to a family of free Negroes. She had been hidden in the attic of the home of a Quaker. She had been befriended by stout German farmers, whose guttural speech surprised her

11

and whose well-kept farms astonished her. She had never before seen barns and fences, farmhouses and outbuildings, so carefully painted. The cattle and horses were so clean they looked as though they had been scrubbed.

When she crossed the line into the free state of Pennsylvania, the sun was coming up. She said, 'I looked at my hands to see if I was the same person now I was free. There was such a glory over everything, the sun came like gold through the trees, and over the fields, and I felt like I was in heaven.'

Once in Pennsylvania Harriet made it her business to learn all she could about the extent of the network of stops on the Underground Railroad. By 1851 she had become personally involved in its work. She explained her decision to run the risk of going North alone in these words: 'I had reasoned this out in my mind; there was one of two things I had a *right* to, liberty or death; if I could not have one, I would have the other; for no man should take me alive; I should fight for my liberty as long as my strength lasted, and when the time came for me to go, the Lord would let them take me.'

Though she was not aware of it, she soon became a legend in the slave cabins along the Eastern shore. She had always had the makings of a legend in her: the prodigious strength, the fearlessness, the religious ardour, the visions she had in which she experienced moments of prescience. Stories about her would be handed down from on generation to the next, embroidered, embellished, until it would be impossible to say which part was true, which part was fiction. But each one who heard the stories, each one who told all of them, or only parts of them, would feel stronger because of her existence. Pride in her would linger on in the teller of the story as well as the listener. Their faith in a living God would be strengthened, their faith in themselves would be renewed.

The slaves said she could see in the dark like a mule, that she could smell danger down the wind like a fox, that she could move through thick underbush without making a sound, like a field mouse. They said she was so strong she could pick up a grown man, sling him over her shoulder and walk with him for miles.

They said, voices muted, awed, that she talked with God

every day, just like Moses. They said there was some strange power in her so that no one could die when she was with them. She enveloped the sick and the dying with her strength, sending it from her body to theirs, sustaining them.

They changed her name again. At first she had been called Minta or Minty. After her defiance of the overseer, they called her Harriet, because the pet names, the diminutives, were no longer fitting for a girl who had displayed such courage.

Now they called her Moses.

Under her guidance, over three hundred slaves reached the North and freedom. By 1860 the rewards offered for her capture totalled sixty thousand dollars.

With the onset of the American Civil War, Harriet changed her role. The Confederate forts had been taken on November 7, 1861, and Port Royal and St. Helena were being used by the Union Army as supply stations. Slaves had been flocking to these islands ever since the Union forces had set up headquarters there. These slaves were referred to as "contrabands." The term originated from an army report of May 24, 1861. Three fugitives were brought into Fortress Monroe by the Union picket guard. The Confederates asked for their rendition under the terms of the Fugitive Slave Law, but they were informed by General Butler that "under the peculiar circumstances, he considered the fugitives 'contraband' of war."

Port Royal was filled with contrabands, poverty stricken, sick, homeless, starving. Many of them had travelled miles from the interior of South Carolina in order to reach the Union headquarters on the island. Some of them had been wounded by plantation owners who had attempted to halt their flight. A hospital had been set up for them on Port Royal.

It was in this contraband hospital that Harriet Tubman began to play her new role of nurse. She said, 'I'd go to the hospital, I would, early every morning. I'd get a big chunk of ice, I would, and put it in a basin, and fill it with water, then I'd take a sponge and begin. First man I'd come to, I'd thrash away the flies, and they'd rise, they would, like bees around a hive. Then I'd begin to bathe the wounds, and by the time I bathed off three or four, the fire and heat would have melted the ice and made the water warm, and it would be as red as clear blood. Then I'd go and get more ice, I would, and by the time I got to the next ones, the flies would be around the first ones black and thick as ever.'

More deadly than the wounds was the dysentery. Each morning when she went back to the hospital, she found more and more people had died from it. She was certain she could check it if she could find the same roots and herbs here on the island that had grown in Maryland. But this was a strange new country to her; even the plant life was different.

One night she went into a wooded area, near the water, and searched until she found the great white flowers of the water lily floating on the surface, reached down and pulled up the roots, hunted until she found crane's bill. Then she went back to the small house where she lived and boiled the roots and herbs, making a strange dark-looking concoction. It was a bitter-tasting brew. But it worked. The next morning she gave it to a man who was obviously dying, and slowly he got better.

Once again men called her Moses, saying that no one could die if Moses was at the bedside.

In January, 1863, shortly after Lincoln had proclaimed the slaves free, she saw a regiment of Negro soldiers for the first time. Thomas Wentworth Higginson, their commanding officer, was an old friend of Harriet's. As Harriet wached these men parade through the sandy streets, shaded by the tremendous live oaks, one thousand ex-slaves marching in unison, she was overcome by emotion. The band of the Eighth Maine met the regiment at the entrance to Beaufort and escorted them all the way.

She thought this the most moving sight she had ever beheld: a regiment of black, newly-freed South Carolinians wearing the uniform of the Union forces, escorted by the band of a white regiment. She knew how Sergeant Prince Rivers, the six-foot colour sergeant of the First Carolina Volunteers, felt when he said, 'And when that band wheel in before us, and march on—my God! I quit this world altogether.'

About a month later, she started serving as a scout for Colonel James Montgomery, who had encamped at Port Royal with the first detachment of the Second Carolina Volunteers, also composed of ex-slaves. On the night of June 2, 1863,

Harriet accompanied Montgomery and his men in a raid up the Combahee River. They had two objectives: to destroy or take up the torpedoes that the enemy had placed in the Combahee and to bring back to Port Royal as many contrabands as they could entice away from the river area.

They soon found out that they would not have to entice the inhabitants away. As the gunboats went farther and farther up the Combahee, they began to see slaves working in the rice fields. At first the slaves ran away, toward the woods. Then the word was passed around, 'Lincoln's gunboats done come to set us free.'

People started coming toward the boats, coming down the paths, through the meadows, for on each side of the river there were rice fields and slaves working in them. They kept coming, with bundles on their heads, children riding on their mothers' shoulders, all of them ragged, dirty, the children naked.

Harriet said that she had never seen anything like it before. 'Here you'd see a woman with a pail on her head, rice a-smoking in it just as she'd taken it from the fire, young one hanging on behind, one hand round her forehead to hold on, other hand digging into the ricepot, eating with all its might, hold of her dress two or three more down her back a bag with a pig in it.

'One woman brought two pigs, a white one and a black one; we took them all on board; named the white pig Beauregard, and the black pig Jeff Davis. Sometimes the women would come with twins hanging round their necks; appears like I never see so many twins in my life; bags on their shoulders, baskets on their heads, and young ones tagging behind, all loaded; pigs squealing, chickens screaming, young ones squalling.'

They were taken off the shore in rowboats. Even after the boats were crowded, they clung to the sides of them, holding them fast to the shore. The men rowing the boats struck at their hands with the oars, but they would not let go. They were afraid they would be left behind.

Shortly afterward, Harriet had someone write a letter to Franklin B. Sanborn in Boston, asking for a bloomer dress because long skirts were a handicap on an expedition.

Sanborn was at the time editor of *The Boston Commonwealth*. He made a front-page story of the Combahee raid, and Harriet's part in it. It appeared Friday, July 10, 1863: "Col. Montgomery and his gallant band of 300 black soldiers, under the guidance of a black woman, dashed into the enemy's country, struck a bold and effective blow ...and bought off near 800 slaves ..."

"Since the rebellion she [Harriet] has devoted herself to her great work of delivering the bondman, with an energy and sagacity that cannot be exceeded. Many and many times she has penetrated the enemy's lines and discovered their situation and condition, and escaped without injury, but not without extreme hazard ..."

At the end of the war Harriet returned to Auburn to look after her parents. Because she was never granted a pension for her years of service in the Union forces, she had little or no money.

In May of 1868, one of Harriet's friends and admirers, Mrs Sarah Hopkins Bradford, a school-teacher who lived in Auburn, decided to do something to raise some money for her. She began to write the story of Harriet's life. Most of the direct quotations used by biographers of Harriet Tubman are possible only because of Mrs Bradford, who first recorded them.

As she grew older, the pattern of her life changed again. Finally, she became a tiny little old woman, peddling vegetables from door to door in Auburn. She didn't make many stops in the course of a day. There wasn't time. At each house, she was invited inside, told to sit down, and urged to tell a story about some phase of her life. Sometimes she spent the whole morning in one house. The housewife who sat across the kitchen table from Harriet, listening, felt as though she were travelling, too, and so was reluctant to let her go on to her next stop.

It was as the storyteller, the bard, that Harriet's active years came to a close. She had never learned to read or write. She compensated for this handicap by developing a memory on which was indelibly stamped everything she had ever heard or seen or experienced. She had a highly developed sense of the dramatic, a sense of the comic, and because in her early years she had memorised verses from the Bible, word for word, the surge and sway of the majestic rhythm of the King James version of the Bible was an intergral part of her speech. It was these qualities that made her a superb storyteller.

She died on March 10, 1913. Of her old friends and associates, only Sanborn and Higginson were still alive. The others had gone long before. Theodore Parker, Thomas Garrett, William H. Seward, William Lloyd Garrison, Frederick Douglass, Colonel James Montgomery.

In many ways she represented the end of an era, the most dramatic, and the most tragic, era in American history. Despite her work as a nurse, a scout, and a spy, in the Civil War, she will be remembered longest as a conductor on the Underground Railroad, the railroad to freedom—a short, indomitable woman, sustained by faith in a living God, inspired by the belief that freedom was a right all men should enjoy, leading bands of trembling fugitives out of Tidewater Maryland.

On July 12, 1914, the city of Auburn paid tribute to her. During the day flags were flown at half-mast. At night a tremendous mass meeting was held in the Auditorium, where a bronze tablet which had been inscribed to her memory was unveiled. The tablet was placed on the front entrance of the Courthouse in Auburn. This is what it says:

IN MEMORY OF HARRIET TUBMAN.
BORN A SLAVE IN MARYLAND ABOUT 1821.
DIED IN AUBURN, N.Y. MARCH 10TH, 1913.
CALLED THE MOSES OF HER PEOPLE,
DURING THE CIVIL WAR. WITH RARE
COURAGE SHE LED OVER THREE HUNDRED
NEGROES UP FROM SLAVERY TO FREEDOM,
AND RENDERED INVALUABLE SERVICE
AS A NURSE AND SPY.
WITH IMPLICIT TRUST IN GOD
SHE BRAVED EVERY DANGER AND
OVERCAME EVERY OBSTACLE. WITHAL
SHE POSSESSED EXTRAORDINARY
FORESIGHT AND JUDGEMENT SO THAT
SHE TRUTHFULLY SAID
"ON MY UNDERGROUND RAILROAD
I NEBBER RAN MY TRAIN OFF DE TRACK
AN' I NEBBER LOS' A PASSENGER."
THIS TABLET IS ERECTED
BY THE CITIZENS OF AUBURN.

A Belfast Woman

I mind well the day the threatening letter came. It was a bright morning, and warm, and I remember thinking while I was dressing myself that it would be nice if the Troubles were over so that a body could just enjoy the feel of a good day. When I came down the stairs the hall was dark but I could see the letter lying face down. I lifted it and just my name was on the envelope, 'Mrs Harrison' in red felt pen. I knew what it was. There was a page of an exercise book inside with 'Get out or we'll burn you out' all in red with bad printing and smeared. I just went in and sat at the kitchen table with the note in front of me. I never made myself a cup of tea even. It was a shock, though God knows I shouldn't have been surprised.

One of the first things I remember in my life was wakening up with my mother screaming downstairs when we were burnt out in 1921. I ran down in my nightgown and my mother was standing in the middle of the kitchen with her hands up to her face screaming and screaming and the curtains were on fire and my father was pulling them down and stamping on them with the flames catching the oilcloth on the floor. Then he shouted: 'Sadie, the children', and she stopped screaming and said: 'Oh God, Michael, the children', and she ran upstairs and came down with the baby in one arm and Joey under the other, and my father took Joey in his arms and me by the hand and we ran out along the street. It was a warm summer night and the fires were crackling all over the place and the street was covered with broken glass. It wasn't until we got into my grandmother's house that anybody noticed that I had nothing on but my nightie and nothing on my feet and they were cut. It was all burnt, everything they had. My mother used to say she didn't save as much as a needle and thread. I wasn't able to sleep for weeks, afraid I'd be wakened by that screaming.

We stayed in my grandmother's house until 1935 and my grandmother was dead by that time and my father too for he got T.B. like many another then. He used to say 'When you have no house and no job sure what use are you?' and then he'd get fits of coughing. In 1935 when we got the letter threatening to burn us out I said to my mother 'We'll gather our things and we'll go.' So we did and like all the rest of them in our street we went up to Glenard to the new houses. When we showed our 'Get out or we'll burn you out' note they gave us a house and we'd enough out to get things fixed up. We got new jobs in another mill, my mother and Patsy and me. Only my mother never liked it there. She always said the air was too strong for her. It was cold right enough, up close to the mountains. But when I was getting married to William, and his aunt who was a Protestant gave him the key of her house in this street, my mother was in a terrible state — 'Don't go into that Protestant street, Mary, or you'll be a sorry girl,' and she said we could live with her. But I didn't want William to pine like my poor father, so here we came and not a day's trouble until the note came.

Mind you, the second night we were here there was trouble in the Catholic streets across the road. We heard shots first and then the kind of rumbling, roaring noises of all the people out on the streets. I wanted to get up and run out and see what was wrong but William held on to me in bed and he said: 'They don't run out on the street here. They stay in.' And it was true. They did. I was scared lying listening to the noise the way I never was when I was out with my neighbours. It turned out some poor young lad had stayed at home when he should have gone back to the British army and they sent the police for him. He got out of the back window and ran down the entry and the police ran after him and shot him dead. They said their gun went off by accident but the people said they beat him up. When I went over the next day I saw him laid out in the wee room off the kitchen and his face had all big yellowy-greenish blotches on it. I never mentioned it to my new neighbours and they never mentioned it to me.

I couldn't complain about them. They were good decent people. They didn't come into the house for a chat or a loan of tea or milk or sugar like the neighbours in Glenard or North Queen Street but they were ready to help at any time. I didn't know the men much because they had work so they didn't stand around the corners the way I was used to. But when Liam was born they all helped and said what a fine baby he was. He was too. Nine pounds with black hair and so strong he could lift his head and look round at a week old. They were always remarking on his mottled skin — purply kind of measles when he'd be up out of the pram — and said it was the sign of a very strong baby. At that time I had never seen a baby with any other colour of skin — I suppose Catholic babies had to be strong to get by. But when Eileen was born a year and ten months later she was different. She had beautiful creamy skin. She was plump and perfect and I loved her more than Liam, God forgive me, and more than William and more than anybody in the world and I wanted everything to be right for her. I thought to myself if I was a Protestant now we'd have just the two and no more and I'd be able to look after them and do well for them. So I didn't act fair with William at all.

Then I started having trouble. I looked as if I was expecting again and my stomach was hard and round but I had bleeding and I could feel no life so I was afraid. I went to the doctor and he said 'No, Mrs Harrison, you're not pregnant. There is something here we shall have to look into.' And I said 'Is it serious, doctor?' and he said 'I can't tell you that, can I, until you go into hospital and have it investigated' and I said 'Do you mean an operation?' and he said 'I do, Mrs Harrison.' I came home saying to myself it's cancer and who will rear my Eileen and Liam. I remembered hearing it said that once they put the knife into you, you were dead in six months so I made up my mind I'd have no operation and I'd last out as long as I could. Every year I was able to look after them would be a year gained

and the bigger they were the better they'd be able to do without me. But oh dear it was terrible hard on everybody. I told
William and my mother and Patsy there was nothing at all the
matter with me but they knew to look at me it wasn't true. I
was a real blay colour and I was so tired I was ready to drop.
I'd sit down by the fire at night when the children were in bed
and my eyes would close and if I opened them I'd see William
staring at me with such a tortured look on his face I'd have to
close them again so that I wouldn't go and lean my head
against him and tell him the whole thing. I knew if I did that
he'd make me go back to the doctor and I'd be done for. At
times I'd see against my closed eyes the white long roots of the
cancer growing all over my inside and I'd remember the first
time William brought me to see his father in the country.

He had a fine labourer's cottage for he was a Protestant and
was head ploughman to some rich farmer down there. He was
a good man. William's mother was a Catholic and she died
when William was a wee boy but they brought him up a
Catholic because it had been promised. He was cross-looking
though, and I was a bit nervous of him. He had his garden all
planted in rows and squares and he was digging clods in one
corner and breaking them up fine and I could see all the long
white roots and threads he was shaking the mud out of and he
turned to us and he said: 'Sitfast and scutch! Sitfast and scutch!
They're the plague of my life. No matter how much I weed
there's more in the morning.' I told him about my grandfather
and the big elderberry tree that grew behind the wee house
he'd got in the country when he was burnt out in Lisburn. It
wasn't there when he went into the house and when he
noticed it first it was only a wee bit of a bush but it grew so
quickly it blocked out all the light from his back window. Then
one summer it was covered with black slimy kind of flies so he
cut it down to the stump, but it started growing again straight
away. One day when my father took Patsy and Joey and me
down to visit him he had dug all around the stump and he was
trying to pull it out with a rope. He told my father to pull with
him. My father tried but then he leaned against the wall with
his face pale and covered with sweat. My grandfather said:
'Are you finished, Michael,' and my father said 'I'm clean

21

done,' and my grandfather said 'God help us all' and brought us into the house and gave us lemonade. It was just after that my father went into the sanatorium and my mother was all the time bringing him bottles of lemonade. At the funeral I asked my grandfather if he got the stump out and he didn't know for a minute what I was talking about. Then he said 'No, no. Indeed the rope's still lying out there. I must bring it in or it'll rot.' I never saw him again, never saw the wee house either. My mother never was one for the country.

She wasn't old herself when she died — not that much over fifty, but she looked an old woman. She wore a shawl at times and not many did that any more. She was always fussing about my health and me going to the doctor but I managed fine without. I didn't look much. I had this swollen stomach and I got into the way of hiding it with my arms. But every year I got through I'd say to myself wasn't I right to stick it out. When the war finished and the free health came, everybody thought I'd get myself seen to, and my mother was at me she'd mind Liam and Eileen. Of course there were no more children but I kept those two lovely. There was no Protestant child better fed or better dressed than those two, and I always warned them to fight with nobody, never to get into trouble. If any of the children started to shout at them about being Catholics or Fenians or Teagues they were just to walk away, not to run mind you, but just to walk home. And Liam was the best boy ever. He wasn't great at his lesson but the masters said how pleasant and good he was. Eileen was inclined to be a bit bold and that was the cause of the only terrible thing I ever did. I can't believe even now how I came to do it. It was the week after my mother had died.

I blamed myself for what happened to my mother. I should have seen in time that she wasn't well and made her mind herself and she'd have lasted better. She came into my house one day with her shawl on and I was going to say I wished she'd wear a coat and not have my neighbours passing remarks, but she hung the shawl up on the back of the door and she looked poorly. She said she'd had a terrible pain in her chest and she had been to the doctor and he'd told her it was her heart. She was to rest and take tablets. She had other wee tablets to put under her tongue if she got a pain and she was not to go up hills. She looked so bad I put her to bed in the wee room off the kitchen. She never got up again. She had tense crushing pains and the tablets did no good. Sometimes the sip of Lourdes water helped her. The doctor said he could do nothing for her unless she went into hospital and she wouldn't hear of that. 'Ah no, no. I'm just done, that's all.' Every now and again she'd say this would never have happened if she hadn't been burnt out of her home down near the docks and had to go half roads up the mountains with all the hills and the air too strong for her. 'And your father wouldn't ever have got consumption if he hadn't had to move in with my mother and spend his days at the street corner. You wouldn't remember it, Mary. You were too small' she'd say and I never contradicted her, 'but we hadn't left as much as a needle and thread. The whole block went up. Nothing left.' She was buried from our house even though she kept saying she must go home. She had a horror of my Protestant neighbours even though she liked well enough the ones she met. But at her funeral, better kinder decenter neighbours you could not get. When it was over, all I could do was shiver inside myself as if my shelter had been taken away. William was good to me, always good to me, but I had to keep a bit of myself to myself with him. My mother never looked for anything from me. I'd tell her what I needed to tell her and she'd listen but she never interfered. And she was as proud of Liam and Eileen as I was. I'd see the way she looked at them.

The week after she died Eileen came home from school crying. She was ten years of age and she didn't often cry. She showed me the mark on her legs where the head-teacher had hit her with a cane. A big red mark it was right across the back of her legs. And she had lovely skin on her legs, lovely creamy skin. When I think of it I can still see that mark. I didn't ask her what happened. I just lifted my mother's shawl from where it was still hanging on the back of the kitchen door and I flung it round me and ran down to the school. I knocked the door and she opened it herself, the head-teacher, because the most of the school had gone home. She took one look at me and ran away back into a classroom. I went after her. She ran into another room off it and banged the door. My arm stuck in through the glass panel and I pulled it out with a big deep cut from my wrist to my elbow. She didn't come out of the door and I never spoke to her at all. There were a couple of other teachers over a bit and a few children about but I couldn't say anything to anybody and they just stood. To stop the blood pouring so much I held my arm up out of my mother's shawl as I went back up the street. There was a woman standing at her door near the top of the street. She was generally at her door knitting, that woman. She had very clever children and some of them did well. One got to be a teacher, another was in the Post Office which is about as far as a clever poor Catholic can get. She asked me what happened but when I couldn't answer she said 'You'd need to get to the hospital Mrs. I'll get my coat and go with you.' I didn't want to go to any hospital. I just wanted to go home and wash off all the blood but my head was spinning so I let myself be helped on the bus. They stitched it up and wanted me to stay in for the night but I was terrified they'd operate on me just when I was managing so well. I insisted I couldn't because the children were on their own and Mrs O'Reilly came with me right to the end of my own street. 'If your neighbours ask what happened, just tell them you fell off the bus,' she told me. 'You don't want them knowing all about your business.' I've heard she was from the west of Ireland.

When I went into the kitchen I was ready to drop but Eileen started screaming and crying and saying how ashamed of me she was and that she'd never go back to school again. Liam made me a cup of tea and stood looking worried at me. When William came in from work he helped me to bed and was kind and good but I could see by the cut of his mouth that he was shocked and offended at me. It took a long time to heal and the scar will never leave me. The story went around the parish in different ways. Some said I hit the teacher. Some said she knifed me. I was too ashamed ever to explain.

Eileen never was touched in school after that, though, and when she left she learned shorthand and typing and got an office job. She grew up lovely, and I used to think, watching her going out in the morning in the best of clothes with her hair shining that she could have gone anywhere and done her-self credit. She wasn't contented living where we did. At first I didn't understand what she wanted. I thought she wanted a better house in a better district. I didn't know how we could manage it but I made up my mind it would have to be done. I went for walks up round the avenues where there were detached houses with gardens and when I saw an empty house I'd peer in through the windows. Then one day a woman from the parish, who worked cleaning one of those houses, saw me and asked me in because the people of the house were out all day. Seeing it furnished with good solid shining furniture I knew we'd never manage it. In the sitting-room there was an old-fashioned copper canopy and when I looked into it I could see the whole room reflected smaller like a fairytale with flowers and books and pictures and plates on the wall. I knew it wasn't for us. How could I go in and out there? William and Liam wouldn't look right in their working clothes. Only Eileen would fit in. I was a bit sad but relieved because at no time could I see where the money would have come from. I told her that night when she came in but she looked at me puzzled. 'But that wasn't what I meant, Mammy,' she said. 'I have to get away from everything here. There's no life for me here. I'm thinking of going to Canada.' That was before any trouble at all here. People now would say that was in the good times when you could get in a bus and go round the shops or into the pictures and nothing would have happened by the time you came home except that the slack would have burnt down a bit on the fire.

Off she went anyway and got a job and wrote now and again telling us how well off she was. In no time at all she was mar-ried and was sending photographs first of this lovely bungalow and then of her two wee girls with the paddling pool in her garden or at their swing when they were a bit bigger. I was glad she was doing so well. It was the kind of life I had reared her for and dreamed of for her only I wished she and her chil-dren were not so far away. I kept inviting her home for a visit but I knew it would cost far too much money. Only I thought if she was homesick it would help her to know we wanted to see her too. Once the troubles came I stopped asking her.

Liam at that time was getting on well too. He was always such a nice pleasant big fellow that a plumber in the next street to ours asked him to join in his business at putting in fireplaces and hot water pipes. He put in a lovely fireplace for me with a copper canopy like the one I'd seen years before and built me a bathroom and hot water and put in a sink unit for me till I was far better off than any of my neighbours even though a lot of them had their houses very nice too. They were able to get paint from the shipyard of course, and marble slabs and nice bits of mahogany. He got married to a nice wee girl from the Bone and they got a house up in one of the nice streets in Ardoyne — up the far end in what they call now a mixed area. It's all gone now, poor Liam's good way of living. When that street of houses up there was put on fire in 1972 his wife Gemma insisted on coming back to the Bone and squatting in an empty house. They did their best to fix it up but it's old and dark. Then when the murders got bad his partner asked him not to come back to work any more because he'd been threatened for working with a Catholic. I was raging when Liam told me, raging about what a coward the plumber was but then as Liam said, you can't blame a man for not wanting to be murdered. So there he is — no work and no house and a timid wife and a family of lovely wee children. He had plenty to put up with. But where else could I go when I got the note. I sat looking round my shining kitchen and the note said 'Get out or we'll burn you out' and where could I go for help but to Liam.

Still I was glad William was dead before it happened. He would have been so annoyed. He felt so ashamed when the Protestants did something nasty. I could swallow my own shame every time the I.R.A. disgraced us. I lived with it the same as I lived with the memory of my own disgrace when I went for the teacher and ripped my arm. But William had always been such a good upright man, he could never understand wickedness. Even the way he died showed it. He was a carter all his days, always in steady work but for a while before he died they were saying to him that nobody had horses any more and they were changing to a lorry. He could never drive a lorry. He was afraid he'd be on the dole. It wasn't the money he was worrying about for I kept telling him it would make little difference to us — just the two of us, what did it matter. It was his pride that was upset. For years there was a big notice up on a corner shop at the bottom of the Oldpark Road. It said: 'Drivers, dismount. Don't overload your horses going up the hill.' He used to remark on it. It irked him if he didn't obey it. So one day in March when there was an east wind he collapsed on the hill and died the next day in hospital with the same disease as my mother.

There was a young doctor in the hospital asked me did I need a tranquilliser or a sleeping tablet or something to get over the shock. I told him no that I never took any tablets, that I had had cancer when I was in my twenties and that I was still alive in my fifties with never a day in bed. He was curious and he asked me questions and then he said, 'Mrs Harrison, of course I can't be absolutely sure, but I'd say it was most unlikely you had cancer. Maybe you needed a job done on your womb. Maybe you even needed your womb removed but I would be very, very surprised if you had cancer. You wouldn't be here now if you had.' So I went in and knelt down at William's side. He still had that strained, worried look, even then. All I could think was: 'Poor William. Poor William. Poor, poor, poor William.'

It wasn't that I was lonely without him for I'd kept him at a distance for a long time, but the days had no shape to them. I could have my breakfast, dinner and tea whatever time I liked or I needn't have them at all. For a while I didn't bother cooking for myself, just ate tea and bread. Then Liam's wife, Gemma, said the butcher had told her that I hadn't darkened his door since William died and that if I wouldn't cook for myself I'd have to come and have my dinner with them. So I thought to myself I wasn't being sensible and I'd only be a nuisance to them if I got sick so I fixed everything to the clock as if there was no such thing as eternity. Until that morning the note came and then I just sat, I didn't look at the clock. I didn't make a cup of tea. I didn't know how long I stayed. I felt heavy, not able to move. Then I though maybe Liam could get somebody with a van to take out my furniture and I could think later where to go. I took my Rosary beads from under my pillow and my handbag with my money and my pension book and Eileen's letters and the photographs of her children and I shut the door behind me. There wasn't a soul in the street but there was nothing odd about that. You'll always know you're in a Protestant street if it's deserted. When I went across the road to get to Liam's house there were children playing and men at the corner and women standing at the doors in the sun and a squad of nervous-looking soldiers down at the other end.

Liam wasn't in but Gemma and the children were. The breakfast table wasn't cleared and Gemma was feeding the youngest. When he finished she stood him up on her lap and he reached over her shoulder trying to reach the shiny new handle Liam had put on the door. He was sturdy and happy and he had a warm smell of milk and baby-powder. I wanted to hold him but I was afraid of putting her out of her routine. Sometimes I wonder if she has a routine — compared to the way I reared mine. Nothing was allowed to interrupt their feeding times and sleeping times. Maybe I was wrong and I'll never know what way Eileen managed hers. I would have liked to do the dishes too but I was afraid it might look like criticising. After a wee while chatting Gemma got up to put the child in his pram and make us a cup of tea. 'You don't look great, Granny,' she said. 'Are you minding yourself at all?' I opened my bag and showed her the note.

She screamed and put her hands up to her face and the baby was startled and cried and bounced up and down in his pram with his arms up to be lifted. I said 'Don't scream, Gemma. Don't ever scream, do you hear me,' and I unstrapped the baby and hugged him. She stared at me, surprised, and it stopped her. 'You'll have to come and stay here,' she said. 'We'll fit you in.' She gave a kind of a look around and I could see her thinking where on earth she could fit me in. Still where could I go? 'All I wanted was for Liam to get a van and take out my stuff,' I explained. 'Maybe my sister Patsy would have more room than you.' She took the baby and gave me my cup of tea. 'You'll come here,' she said. 'You'll count this your home and we'll be glad to have you.' She was a good kind girl, Gemma, and when Liam came in he was the same; only anxious to make me welcome and he went off to get the van.

After a while Gemma said 'Write to Eileen straight away. She's the one you should be living with anyway — not all alone over yonder. All her money and her grand house. She's the one should have you.' I laughed but it hurt me a bit to hear it said. 'What would I do in Eileen's grand house in Canada? How would I fit in?' And Gemma said: 'You could keep her house all shining. She'd use you for that. Where would you see the like of your own house for polish! You'd do great for Eileen.' I looked round her own few bits and pieces — no look on anything, and a pile of children's clothes on the floor waiting to be washed and the children running in and out and knocking things over. Mary, my wee Godchild, came and stood leaning against my knees, sucking her thumb. She was wearing one of the dresses I make for them. In the spring when I was fitting it on her I was noticing how beautiful her skin was with little pinprick freckles on the pink and white and I was thinking when she's so lovely what must Eileen's children be like. Then she turned her head and looked at me and her eyes were full of love — for me! I couldn't get over it. Since then sometimes she'd just hold my hand. When Liam came back I said, 'Liam, I'm going home. I'm sorry about the bother. I just got frightened but you can cancel the van. I'm going home and I'm staying home. I've a Protestant house to the right of me and a Protestant house to the left of me. They'll not burn me out.' They argued with me and they were a bit upset but I knew they were relieved and I stuck to it.

Liam insisted on going back to the house with me although since the murders started I had never let him come down my side of the road. There was a land-rover with soldiers in it not far from my door and no flames, no smoke. But when I opened the door, such a mess. There was water spouting out of a broken pipe in the wall where they had pulled out my sink. The Sacred Heart statue and the wee red lamp were broken on the floor. My copper canopy was all dinged. The table had big hatchet marks on it. The cover on the couch was ripped and the stuffing pulled out. And filth. For months I thought I could get the smell of that filth. I wouldn't let Liam turn off the water until I had washed it away. We cleaned up a bit but Liam said he'd have to get help before he could do much and not to touch the electric because the water had got into it. He had been very quiet so I jumped when he shouted at the soldiers once he went out the door. They drove up very slowly and he was shouting and waving his arms and calling them names. One of them looked into the house and started to laugh. Liam yelled at him about me being a widow woman living alone and that they were here to protect me but one of them said, 'You've got it wrong. We're here to wipe out the I.R.A.'

'Oh, Liam', I said, 'go home. Go home before harm befalls you,' and he shook his fist at the soliders and shouted, 'I'm going now but I'll be back and I won't be on my own then. Just look out. I'm warning you.' He turned and ran off down the street and the solider turned and looked after him and I thought he was lifting up his gun and I grabbed at his arm and the gun went off into the air and I begged, 'Don't shoot at him. Oh don't shoot him.' He said, 'Mrs I have no intention...' and then I fell against the wall and when I came to they were making me drink whiskey out of a bottle. It made me cough and splutter but it brought me round. They weren't bad to me I must admit. When I was on my feet they corked up the bottle and put it back in the landrover and drove off. Not one of my neighbours came out and all evening when I worked at tidying up and all night when I sat up to keep watch, not one of them knocked at my door.

Next day Liam brought back two other lads and they fixed up the electricity and the water. It took a while to get everything decent again but they were in and out every day, sometimes three or four of them and it never cost me a penny. Then a queer thing happened. My neighbours began moving out. The woman next door told me out of the side of her mouth that they had all been threatened. I didn't understand how a whole Protestant area could be threatened but out they all went. Of course I know they can always get newer better houses when they ask for them and indeed there was a lot of shooting and wrecking on the front of the road, but still I often wondered what was the truth of it. Maybe I'm better off not knowing. As they left, Catholics from across the road moved in — mostly older people and I have good friends among them although it took us a while to get used to each other. I didn't take easy to people expecting to open my door and walk in at any hour of the day. They thought I was a bit stiff. I have no time for long chats and I never liked gossip. But Mrs Mulvenna, next door now, has a son in Australia — farther away than my Eileen and I think sons are even worse at writing home. I listen to her and I feel for her and I show her my photographs. I didn't tell her when Eileen wrote about how ashamed she was of us all and how she didn't like to let on she was Irish. I see talk like that in the papers too. It's not right to put the blame on poor power-less people. The most of us never did anything but stay quiet and put up with things the way they were. And we never taught our children to hate the others nor filled their heads with their wrongs the way it's said we did. When all the young people thought they could fix everything with marches and meetings I said it wouldn't work and they laughed at me. 'All you old ones are awful bitter,' they said and they jeered when Hannah in the shop and I were warning them 'It'll all lead to shooting and burning and murder.'

Still, last November a man came round here trying to sell Venetian blinds. Some of the houses have them but I said no I liked to see out. I pointed to the sunset behind Divis — bits of red and yellow in the sky and a sort of mist all down the mountain that made it nearly see-through. The man looked at it for a minute and then he said, 'Do you know Belfast has the most beautiful sunsets in the whole world?' I said I didn't because I'd never been any place close to look at sunsets and he said, 'They tell me Belfast has the best and do you know why? It's because of all the smoke and dirt and dust and pollution. And it seems to me,' he said, 'it seems to me that if the dirt and dust and smoke and pollution of Belfast just with the help of the sun can make a sky like that, then there's hope for all of us.' He nodded and winked and touched his hat and went off and I went in and sat down at the table. And thinking of it I started to laugh, for it's true. There is hope for all of us. Well anyway, if you don't die you live through it, day in, day out.

My Army Life

Everything happened exactly as we had hoped. After a month and four days the war came to a sudden conclusion, and we came back to Wu Chang singing songs of victory. This West Punitive Expedition cost us more than seventy schoolmates and about a hundred comrades from the training troops. We captured many thousand rifles, and established the foundations of our Revolution in the heart of every citizen of that district. That was an unshakable monument for our cause. The greatest victory for us was that we had delivered from the hands of the military lords thousands and tens of thousands of oppressed people, who now would have a clear understanding of the Revolution and of our cause. We had sown the seeds of revolution in every place we passed. Victory! That was the final victory that we brought home.

One night, seven days after our return from the front, suddenly I heard the bugle. It was a moonless night, but there were a few sparkling stars in the sky. I was sitting with a group of women soldiers talking in the room of the head nurse, who was telling us her happy experiences during the expedition.

As we always did, within three minutes all of us were gathered in formation and had numbered off. We all looked at the five officers who were standing on the platform. They looked downcast, and we did not know what was the trouble. The lieutenant began:

'My schoolmates— ' Strange, that was not his usual saluta-
tion to us. Even his voice was different. Before he went on any
further we seemed to feel that he was trembling. We feared
that something very unfortunate had happened, and sure
enough he was proclaiming our unlucky fate. Indeed, he was
reading out our sentence.

'First of all, I want you to be calm, to be brave, to be prepared
for the worst.'

'What, are we going to the front again? But what is there to
be afraid of?' That was in my thoughts.

'It is very unfortunate news I am going to tell you, but I want
you not to be heart-broken. A revolutionary must be prepared
for set-backs and obstacles. They are quite common. We shall
never give up and never be despairing.'

What was he going to say?

'Because the reactionary force is so great and because we want
to preserve our revolutionary forces for a better time under better circumstances, and because the present conditions are pressing upon us, we have to demobilise for the time being.'

This was a thunderbolt from the blue, a bombshell in the
night! It had almost knocked the life out of all of us. We were
almost unconscious, but the lieutenant's voice went on heroic-
ally:

'Of course, this is not because we are afraid, not because we
do not want to resist, for we are determined to have the final
struggle. Those of you who are very robust and can run very
fast may follow the Eleventh Army to fight. Otherwise you
should all return to your own homes and suffer for the time
being. In the very near future perhaps you will have a freer
and happier life. Now each of you will receive ten silver dollars
for your expenses, and I advise you to get some civilian
clothes to disguise yourselves. The uniforms you must
destroy.'

Heavens, what was this all about? Why should we be
demobilised? Our hopes, our ideals, were they finished after
such a short appearance?

After the lieutenant's report all the other four officers gave
us some further advice, and their words made a very deep
impression on our minds. One of them said:

'If you only hold your belief very firmly in your minds, if you can only think of revolution and sacrifice constantly, then, even if you cannot do anything at present, even if you have to stoop to compromise for a time, so long as you do not forget our great cause, you will eventually wipe out the military lords. All those who have been trained to be soldiers should be brave women and prepared to serve our cause in future.'

These words were sharp as knives piercing into our hearts, and many of us were shedding tears. So we were to leave the school tomorrow! Tomorrow was the time when we should go into hell, for going back to our old-fashioned homes was as bad as going to hell. Alas, who wanted to go there?

During that whole night none of us went to bed. We stood on the training ground shouting slogans, singing and making speeches until daylight came. On the following day all the local girls went home in their beautiful dresses instead of in uniform, and I prepared to return to Changsha.

Because it would be easier for us to make them ourselves, I, Shu Yun, Shiang Shiao and San San bought some white linen to make Western frocks. I say Western frocks not because they were at all like the fashionable garments worn by European ladies, but just plain frocks without buttons, which were very easy to put on—you simply slipped them over your head.

Our hair had been cut very short, especially Shu Yun's, who had shaved her head, making it look very much like a bald pate, and because of that, no matter what masterly disguise she assumed, one could tell at a glance that she was a woman soldier and had carried a rifle. Then, too, we were all sun-tanned and our skins were very dark, and because we had been handling rifles for such a long period, our hands gave us away immediately.

'Our uniforms are gone, when shall we wear them again?' When I said this with a sigh and with tear-drops running down my face, Shu Yun could not suppress her loud sobs. When we looked at the new dresses we had just made, we were very much like mourners who were present at a funeral. We were silent, and very reluctant to change into them. We loved our uniform, and especially the leather belt, which we had rubbed so hard to make it shine. We really did not like to part with that. We remembered that when we had buckled it on the first time, we had thought it nonsense. It was hard and made our waist feel stiff and uncomfortable, so that when we were dismissed the first thing we did was to unbuckle the belt and give our waist a good exercising. Sometimes when we were in a hurry we forgot to buckle the belt as we went on to the drill ground, and because of that we had often been upbraided by our officers. By and by we got used to it, and except when we went to bed, we never left it off for a moment. We had fallen in love with that and our rifle, and, especially in winter time, the belt was a great help to us because it prevented the cold wind from piercing into our bodies. Our rifle, of course, was more dear to us than our lives. The destruction of the old system and the creation of a new society depended upon it.

But now everything was gone. Not only could we not take our rifle with us, but even the little leather belt had to be given up. Alas, alas!

This great, majestic women's army was now demobilised, but the spirit of the movement would live for ever. In 1927 the seeds of revolution had already been sown all over China. In every city and in every village I believed that in future the flowers of revolution would spring up, and final victory would certainly be ours!

Her Story

Maria' story.

My mother had a stroke when she was forty-eight which left her paralysed down one side. In those days, there were no home helps, no auxilaries to come out and give you a hand to wash and dress her and you had all the washing to do yourself. There were practically no social services and you were expected to look after her, even though *you* were disabled. It was a daughter's duty. At the time I already had rheumatoid arthritis and although I could walk around I could only do it with great difficulty. The amount of washing I had to do was quite considerable, and in those days again there weren't things like automatic washing machines, even if you had the money, which we didn't. My mother had worked but there wasn't a great deal in the way of social benefits as there are today, so that we had very little to provide all the necessaries. A washing machine wasn't considered necessary. You were supposed to wash sheets and get them dried and put them on the bed, that was the normal way. So I got absolutely exhausted, I went down to just under six stones in weight, because I looked after her. She was my mother and there was no question of trying to put her away. Even if I had wanted to put her into care, at that time there was no way you could do it, it was a daughter's duty to look after her parents. A daughter didn't have a life of her own. When she died I got a job, not anything very glamorous but at least I did earn my own living, and this was the great thing. I think people don't realise the amount of dignity you get out of having a wage packet. I can remember getting a job in old money for £3 a week, and I had been getting £2.17s.6d. a week dole, so I was working for less than half a crown a week, but it was *my* money. *I'd* worked for it. One of the things I find very irritating is that people tend to look at you as you are now, in a chair, and they think that you've always lived on the state, but that's not true, there's an awful lot of disabled people who have worked, and worked very hard. We've worked at jobs that nobody else would take, low-paid, dirty, unpleasant jobs. There seems to be two standards of living, one for the non-disabled and one for the disabled, and the thing is, what is for the disabled will do, but if you're not disabled, it won't do for you. People seem to be surprised that you have a standard, because perhaps you can't get washed yourself, so they think it doesn't really matter, but I like my dignity, I want to be as clean and as smart as anybody else, and I find it very irritating. I'm only human, I haven't a lot going for me, but what I've got I like to make the most of, like every woman. They seem to think that because you're disabled you have no feelings, no emotions, nothing, you're just like a robot.

I met my husband at a club for disabled people, and this is another thing, that disabled people don't have a great deal of social life. People tend to think that they can put all the disabled together. Now you can put a group of doctors or a group of nurses or any kind of people together, it doesn't mean to say that because they've got one profession they're all going to get on together, and it's the same with disabled people, we're people first and disabled second. So that's how I met my husband. He has now unfortunately developed senile dimentia, which is a very difficult disability to cope with for those who have to look after them. He became doubly incontinent, very confused, and rather difficult to deal with. If he smoked he would drop lighted matches about and set the place on fire, so he had to be taken into care eighteen months ago, but I go and see him every day. He'd had paralysis when he was a little boy, so he's got a double handicap now.

When we got married it was a dirty joke. This is what I mean about they don't think you have the same emotions, the same desires or worries, as able-bodied people. You fall in love, you love somebody, you don't see the disability in them you just see the person. You don't see the crutches, or sticks, or calipers, or wheelchairs, you see a man, and like most women when they meet a man they like, you only see the good points in them. They would say to you, 'What are you getting married *for*?' in a rather sleazy, dirty attitude. The kinds of questions that strangers would ask, people that you didn't know very well — 'What will you do if you have a family?' 'What sort of a sex life will you have?' — I wouldn't think that they'd ask able-bodied couples things like that, and my husband's rather shy, he found it very distressing. I found it just annoying, your whole life is public, you haven't to have any privacy, they like to know every little detail of your life.

As a woman, naturally I wanted children, but we made the decision not to because we didn't think it would be fair on the child. But we still had emotional feelings, we still gave each other strength and companionship, and a lot of people don't understand that, they think that you have got to be sort of producing and it wasn't quite nice for disabled people to produce children. Well that's up to the disabled person, if they want to go ahead and have a family it's got nothing to do with anybody else. What I had wasn't hereditary but there's more to children than having a baby. You see if we'd had children we both would have liked to take them to the country and shown them wild flowers, wild life, taken them to the coast and had picnics, take them bathing, do all the normal things that families do. Love by itself isn't enough for a child, it's got to have experiences, it's got to learn and to grow emotionally as well as physically and that would have been impossible with us. So in a way, we loved our children too much to have them. We sacrificed our children, so that although they wouldn't have a future they weren't going to have a rotten future with two disabled parents hanging round their neck. I don't think you have children to comfort you in your old age, yes of course, you expect that when you have children and you have a good relationship then you want them to come to you when you're ill or you're getting a bit old and you need some moral support, but you don't have them to sacrifice the children to your life, that isn't what having children is about, I don't think it is. I think that partly comes from my experience looking after my mother and when I've looked around and seen people, women, who because they've been the only daughter, or they've been the daughter who isn't married they are expected to sacrifice their lives to look after parents and sometimes the parents live so long because they're well looked after. By the time they die the daughters are so worn out there's no life left for them, and this is wrong, you don't have families for that, or I don't think you should. What is the alternative? — and really women are blackmailed. As a woman I feel that I'm even now emotionally blackmailed sometimes into doing something that's really beyond my strength but I've still got to find the strength from somewhere to do it. Things like going to see my husband, I go up every day, he's dependent on me, he gets very distressed if I don't go up. People still think that I should go on giving myself, even though he isn't at home. It isn't that I don't want to give of myself, but we can all only give so much, and we do have a life, and so often we have to suppress our own feelings, I think, and this is where I think we're emotionally blackmailed because in a way I think we're brainwashed into thinking we should do it.

When I had to give up work, it was after my pelvis twisted and it left me with one leg shorter than the other, the doctor said I would never walk again and they wanted me to go into care. I felt dreadful when I had to give up work, it was the most shattering experience I had had, because going out to work, you felt part of society, you were contributing, you were earning your own money. You also had your friends that you went to work with, and then suddenly you were cut off, you were in the house alone. Also of course you were financially worse off. You were lonely, you felt useless, on the scrap heap, finished, and it really was a very bad time. It wasn't only the idea that you could no longer work, it was the worry of what was going to happen to you, I wasn't married, had no family, no relations. What was going to happen to me? I was frightened. I thought it was the end of the world. Of course it wasn't, that's one thing about disablement, you do learn that you have a crisis but come through it, and so you seem to stagger from crisis to crisis, but you do get through. It is important for women to be able to work, I know you're needed when you're a housewife and at home, but you also have a social need, you want to be out and part of life, because life goes over very quickly and you want to mix with your own generation, there's something that you don't get at home that you get outside at work.

I married about five years after that, and slowly I got back on to my feet. I had one leg shorter that the other but I could get around. We were married for about seven or eight years when I became ill and then it was just impossible for me to think of working again. When I got out of bed, both legs had just gone, and again, you see, I thought that was the end of the world because nobody thinks they can live from a wheelchair, but by gum you can, you can do a lot from a wheelchair. I think there's a great lack of counselling for people who become disabled and have to go into wheelchairs, I don't mean people who just have a limp, I mean really disabled people. Up to a point of course, you have to get through on your own, it's your own personal decision which way you take it, but I think if only there was somebody who would understand the frustrations, the way you feel, your anger, your bad temper, your aggression. There's nothing worse than somebody who's fit and healthy slapping you on your back and saying 'You'll cope' and you look at them and think 'What the hell do they know about it, they're walking around!' but you can take it from somebody else who's in a chair because they've gone through it and they know.

I think disabled people are not used enough. I think that many disabled people do become lethargic, lazy, couldn't care less, and it is not always their fault. They become this way because so often it is quicker for the able-bodied to push them out of the way, to push a wheelchair along, to do things for us, till you come to a point where no matter how strong-willed you are, you give up, you say 'Let them get on with it'. But I think there is a great source of energy, not really physical energy, but mental energy that isn't being tapped, and I think we could relieve able-bodied people by this energy, because we *could* do counselling, we *could* understand. We understand the way disabled people think. So often you get committees, you get all those people who, I know it sounds dreadful, they think they are doing so much good, but they never stop and think 'Right, what do the disabled themselves think?' They go ahead with all these magnificent plans, and of course as far as we're concerned it's a right mess up, and then when you say something, they get really very hurt that you are criticising all their hard work, which I can understand, but if only they would have stopped first and said 'Let's consult the disabled' because we're not all idiots! I don't think things are changing, not a lot, there are some areas where it's a bit better, but I still find the tendancy for a lot of people to shut the disabled out, or what is just as insulting, like the statutory woman, have a disabled person on sufferance, but they don't really want to know what you think, they just want you there to make the numbers up and just be seen.

Clothing is getting to be quite a problem for me because as my physical condition gets worse I am finding it rather difficult to manoeuvre clothes. It does annoy me when a well-meaning occupational therapist says, 'Well, get a size bigger.' I don't want to look like something that's come off a dustcart. I want my clothes to fit, it's important to me to look nice, as nice as I can. I'm not going to sit around looking like something that's come up from a jumble sale. Why should I? Would any other woman? The electric wheelchair improves things — one of the advantages of shopping with the chair is that there's nobody behind me when I choose what I want. There's none of this 'What does she want, what colour does she want?' That happens when you're being pushed around by someone. This is a common complaint amongst disabled people in chairs. They always say the assistant *will* ask the person who's doing the pushing, as though you were a halfwit. I find it marvellous that I can go into a shop and buy a pair of tights for 25p or a three-piece suit for £25 and nobody knows but me how much it cost, where I got it from, and this is great. It gives you such a great feeling it's just between you and the shop, how much you paid for it. Before that, somebody knew, and no matter how good a friend you are, you don't always want them to know how much you pay for all the things you buy. It's your privilege to tell them or not to tell them, but when they're standing there and they know exactly what you've spent, this is part of the thing that I don't like. Especially for disabled women, it's just not expected that you want any sort of privacy in your life at all. The home help goes to the post office, she gets your money, she takes your rent, so she knows how much you've got coming in and how much rent you pay, it isn't really that I want to be secretive, but I do want just that little bit that somebody doesn't know about. It's private and it's part of me—it's like living in a goldfish bowl that everybody can see and know what you're doing. I think we all need to have that little bit of ourselves that's shut away, that nobody else knows about.

I get a bit despondent with the way things are, and they don't seem to be getting any better. I think that one of the things I would like to see changing is the attitude to aids which are very important for disabled people. The powers-that-be, like the local authority, have a set idea of what there is. They haven't got a wide enough horizon. With the silicon chip coming there are going to be many more so-called luxury goods but they're going to be fantastic for disabled people. But local authorities don't want to know because they are luxury goods that only rich women should have. I wonder if it would be the same if I was a man. I need a different kind of telephone in the bedroom but if I had it put in, it would cost me £10 per quarter more because it's a luxury! The very fact that it is a necessity for me doesn't come into it, it's a luxury. I'm fortunate I suppose because I've got a dishwasher, not because they're a luxury but because my hands are too bad to wash dishes. And people say, 'Oh, fancy you having a dishwasher' and 'Aren't you lucky, I can't afford one.' And I know it's not very nice but I say 'Tell you what, give me your hands and you can have my dishwasher' and they take offence, but why should they if I'm not supposed to take offence at being told that I've got luxuries? People still expect you to live on a lower level and if you're a disabled woman, somehow, you're supposed to cope, you're not supposed to get tired, bad-tempered or frustrated or want to throw something through the window. You're not supposed to do it, you're a woman, and that's your job, and you're supposed to have some inner strength and you can go on and on and on.

I think disabled men get supported more, I know by experience, I've seen men who were not half as disabled as a lot of women and my goodness they're run after hand and foot, because 'It's not nice, it takes their dignity away,' that a *man* has been disabled, that a *man* has been the breadwinner and therefore it's a tragedy if he becomes disabled. If a housewife becomes disabled, she's somehow expected to carry on, it's not a tragedy. In some people's eyes it's a bigger tragedy because if a woman is taken out of a house, that house will collapse. A man, I know you miss his money, you miss the man but let's face it, how many women have to cope on their own, not only cope on their own but cope with a disability and very often children. It's very surprising how many men just can't face the fact that their wives are disabled and they just go off and leave them with the kids and all to fend for themselves. I think that's very common—I know quite a few women who've been left in the lurch just because they've become disabled, and yet I know women who have stuck to their husbands and wrecked their own health looking after severely disabled husbands and in turn the women are now really disabled themselves and they've gone on years and years and years, long after they should have given in and said 'I can no longer cope.' I tried to cope for too long quite frankly and I thought that when my husband did go away I would get my strength back but it isn't working out that way. I've spent that strength and there's no way I'm going to get it back. But you see you were his wife and you were expected to cope, as a woman that was part of being married, and to me it isn't, there should be equal shares. I don't want more shares than anybody else, but I want my share of rights, I want my share of dignity and compassion and there's not a lot of it around for women.

A Jury of Her Peers

SUSAN GLASPELL

When Martha Hale opened the storm-door and got a cut of the north wind, she ran back for her big woolen scarf. As she hurriedly wound that round her head her eye made a scandalised sweep of her kitchen. It was no ordinary thing that called her away—it was probably farther from ordinary than anything that had ever happened in Dickson County. But what her eye took in was that her kitchen was in no shape for leaving: her bread all ready for mixing, half the flour sifted and half unsifted.

She hated to see things half done; but she had been at that when the team from town stopped to get Mr Hale, and then the sheriff came running in to say his wife wished Mrs Hale would come too—adding, with a grin, that he guessed she was getting scarey and wanted another woman along. So she had dropped everything right where it was.

'Martha!' now came her husband's impatient voice. 'Don't keep folks waiting out here in the cold.'

She again opened the storm-door, and this time joined the three men and the one woman waiting for her in the big two-seated buggy.

After she had the robes tucked around her she took another look at the woman who sat beside her on the back seat. She had met Mrs Peters the year before at the county fair, and the thing she remembered about her was that she didn't seem like a sheriff's wife. She was small and thin and didn't have a strong voice. Mrs Gorman, sheriff's wife before Gorman went out and Peters came in, had a voice that somehow seemed to be backing up the law with every word. But if Mrs Peters didn't look like a sheriff's wife, Peters made it up in looking like a sheriff. He was to a dot the kind of man who could get himself elected sheriff—a heavy man with a big voice, who was particularly genial with the law-abiding, as if to make it plain that he knew the difference between criminals and non-criminals. And right there it came into Mrs Hale's mind, with a stab, that this man who was so pleasant and lively with all of them was going to the Wrights' now as a sheriff.

'The country's not very pleasant this time of year,' Mrs Peters at last ventured, as if she felt they ought to be talking as well as the men.

Mrs Hale scarcely finished her reply, for they had gone up a little hill and could see the Wright place now, and seeing it did not make her feel like talking. It looked very lonesome this cold March morning. It had always been a lonesome-looking place. It was down in a hollow, and the poplar trees around it were lonesome-looking trees. The men were looking at it and talking about what had happened. The county attorney was bending to one side of the buggy, and kept looking steadily at the place as they drew up to it.

'I'm glad you came with me,' Mrs Peters said nervously, as the two women were about to follow the men in through the kitchen door.

Even after she had her foot on the door-step, her hand on the knob, Martha Hale had a moment of feeling she could not cross that threshold. And the reason it seemed she couldn't cross it now was simply because she hadn't crossed it before. Time and time again it had been in her mind, 'I ought to go over and see Minnie Foster'—she still thought of her as Minnie Foster, though for twenty years she had been Mrs Wright. And then there was always something to do and Minnie Foster would go from her mind. But *now* she could come.

The men went over to the stove. The women stood close together by the door. Young Henderson, the county attorney, turned around and said, 'Come up to the fire, ladies.'

Mrs Peters took a step forward, then stopped. 'I'm not—

45

cold,' she said.

And so the two women stood by the door, at first not even so much as looking around the kitchen.

The men talked for a minute about what a good thing it was the sheriff had sent his deputy out that morning to make a fire for them, and then Sheriff Peters stepped back from the stove, unbuttoned his outer coat, and leaned his hands on the kitchen table in a way that seemed to mark the beginning of official business. 'Now, Mr Hale,' he said in a sort of semi-official voice, 'before we move things about, you tell Mr Henderson just what it was you saw when you came here yesterday morning.'

The county attorney was looking around the kitchen.

'By the way,' he said, 'has anything been moved?' He turned to the sheriff. 'Are things just as you left them yesterday?'

Peters looked from cupboard to sink; from that to a small worn rocker a little to one side of the kitchen table.

'It's just the same.'

'Somebody should have been left here yesterday,' said the county attorney.

'Oh—yesterday,' returned the sheriff, with a little gesture as of yesterday having been more than he could bear to think of. 'When I had to send Frank to Morris Centre for that man who went crazy—let me tell you, I had my hands full *yesterday*. I knew you could get back from Omaha by today, George, and as long as I went over everything here myself—'

'Well, Mr Hale,' said the county attorney, in a way of letting what was past and gone go, 'tell just what happened when you came here yesterday morning.'

Mrs Hale, still leaning against the door, had that sinking feeling of the mother whose child is about to speak a piece. Lewis often wandered along and got things mixed up in a story. She hoped he would tell this straight and plain, and not say unnecessary things that would just make things harder for Minnie Foster. He didn't begin at once, and she noticed that he looked queer—as if standing in that kitchen and having to tell what he had seen there yesterday morning made him almost sick.

'Yes, Mr Hale?' the county attorney reminded.

'Harry and I had started to town with a load of potatoes,' Mrs Hale's husband began.

Harry was Mrs Hale's oldest boy. He wasn't with them now, for the very good reason that those potatoes never got to town yesterday and he was taking them this morning, so he hadn't been home when the sheriff stopped to say he wanted Mr Hale to come over to the Wright place and tell the county attorney his story there where he could point it all out. With all Mrs Hale's other emotions came the fear now that maybe Harry wasn't dressed warm enough—they hadn't any of them realised how that north wind did bite.

'We come along this road,' Hale was going on, with a motion of his hand to the road over which they had just come, 'and as we got in sight of the house I says to Harry, "I'm goin' to see if I can't get John Wright to take a telephone." You see,' he explained to Henderson, 'unless I can get somebody to go in with me they won't come out this branch road except for a price *I* can't pay. I'd spoke to Wright about it once before; but he put me off, saying folks talked too much anyway, and all he asked was peace and quiet—guess you know about how much he talked himself. But I thought maybe if I went to the house and talked about it before his wife, and said all the women-folks like the telephones, and that in this lonesome stretch of road it would be a good thing—well, I said to Harry that that was what I was going to say—though I said at the same time that I didn't know as what his wife wanted made much difference to John —'

Now, there he was!—saying things he didn't need to say. Mrs Hale tried to catch her husband's eye, but fortunately the county attorney interrupted with:

'Let's talk about that a little later, Mr Hale. I do want to talk about that, but I'm anxious now to get along to just what happened when you got here.'

When he began this time, it was very deliberately and carefully:

'I didn't see or hear anything. I knocked at the door. and still it was all quiet inside. I knew they must be up—it was past eight o'clock. So I knocked again, louder, and I thought I heard somebody say "Come in." I wasn't sure—I'm not sure yet. But I opened the door—this door,' jerking a hand toward the door by which the two women stood. 'and there, in that rocker'—pointing to it—'sat Mrs Wright.'

Every one in the kitchen looked at the rocker. It came into Mrs Hale's mind that that rocker didn't look in the least like Minnie Foster—the Minnie Foster of twenty years before. It was a dingy red, with wooden rungs up the back, and the middle rung was gone, and the chair sagged to one side.

'How did she—look?' the county attorney was inquiring.

'Well,' said Hale, 'she looked—queer.'

'How do you mean—queer?'

As he asked it he took out a note-book and pencil. Mrs Hale did not like the sight of that pencil. She kept her eye fixed on her husband, as if to keep him from saying unnecessary things that would go into that note-book and make trouble.

Hale did speak guardedly, as if the pencil had affected him too.

'Well, as if she didn't know what she was going to do next. And kind of—done up.'

'How did she seem to feel about your coming?'

'Why, I don't think she minded—one way or other. She didn't pay much attention. I said, "Ho' do, Mrs Wright? It's cold, ain't it?" And she said, "is it?" — and went on pleatin' at her apron.

'Well, I was surprised. She didn't ask me to come up to the stove, or to sit down, but just set there, not even lookin' at me. And so I said: "I want to see John."

'And then she—laughed. I guess you would call it a laugh.

'I thought of Harry and the team outside, so I said, a little sharp, "Can I see John?" "No," says she—kind of dull like. "Ain't he home?" says I. Then she looked at me. "Yes," says she, "he's home." "Then why can't I see him?" I asked her, out of patience with her now. "Cause he's dead," says she, just as quiet and dull—and fell to pleatin' her apron. "Dead?" says I, like you do when you can't take in what you've heard.

'She just nodded her head, not getting a bit excited, but rockin' back and forth.

'"Why—where is he?" says I, not knowing *what* to say.

'She just pointed upstairs—like this'—pointing to the room above.

'I got up, with the idea of going up there myself. By this time I—didn't know what to do. I walked from there to here; then I says: "Why, what did he die of?"

"He died of a rope around his neck," says she; and just went on pleatin' at her apron.'

Hale stopped speaking, and stood staring at the rocker, as if he were still seeing the woman who had sat there the morning before. Nobody spoke; it was as if every one were seeing the woman who had sat there the morning before.

'And what did you do then?' the county attorney at last broke the silence.

'I went out and called Harry. I thought I might—need help. I got Harry in, and we went upstairs,' His voice fell almost to a whisper. 'There he was—lying over the —'

'I think I'd rather have you go into that upstairs,' the county attorney interrupted, 'where you can point it all out. Just go on now with the rest of the story.'

'Well, my first thought was to get that rope off. It looked —' He stopped, his face twitching.

'But Harry, he went up to him, and he said, "No, he's dead all right, and we'd better not touch anything." So we went downstairs.

'She was still sitting that same way. "Has anybody been notified?" I asked. "No," says she, unconcerned.

'"Who did this, Mrs Wright?" said Harry. He said it business-like, and she stopped pleatin' at her apron. "I don't know," she says. "You don't *know*?" says Harry. "Weren't you sleepin' in the bed with him?" "Yes", says she, "but I was on the inside." "Somebody slipped a rope round his neck and strangled him, and you didn't wake up?" says Harry, "I didn't wake up," she said after him.

'We may have looked as if we didn't see how that could be, for after a minute she said, "I sleep sound."

'Harry was going to ask her more questions, but I said maybe that weren't our business; maybe we ought to let her tell her story first to the coroner or the sheriff. So Harry went fast as he could over to High Road — the Rivers' place, where there's a telephone.'

'And what did she do when she knew you had gone for the coroner?' The attorney got his pencil in his hand all ready for writing.

'She moved from that chair to this one over here'—Hale pointed to a small chair in the corner—'and just sat there with her hands held together and looking down. I got a feeling that I ought to make some conversation, so I said I had come in to see if John wanted to put in a telephone: and at that she started to laugh, and then she stopped and looked at me—scared.'

At the sound of a moving pencil the man who was telling the story looked up.

'I dunno—maybe it wasn't scared,' he hastened; 'I wouldn't like to say it was. Soon Harry got back, and then Dr Lloyd came, and you, Mr Peters, and so I guess that's all I know that you don't.'

He said that last with relief, and moved a little, as if relaxing. Every one moved a little. The county attorney walked toward the stair door.

'I guess we'll go upstairs first—then out to the barn and around there.' He paused and looked around the kitchen.

'You're convinced there was nothing important here?' he asked the sheriff. 'Nothing that would—point to any motive?'

The sheriff too looked all around, as if to re-convince himself.

'Nothing here but kitchen things,' he said, with a little laugh for the insignificance of kitchen things.

The county attorney was looking at the cupboard—a peculiar, ungainly structure, half closet and half cupboard, the upper part of it being built in the wall, and the lower part just the old fashioned kitchen cupboard. As if its queerness attracted him, he got a chair and opened the upper part and looked in. After a moment he drew his hand away sticky.

'Here's a nice mess,' he said resentfully.

The two women had drawn nearer, and now the sheriff's wife spoke.

'Oh—her fruit,' she said, looking to Mrs Hale for sympathetic understanding. She turned back to the county attorney and explained: 'She worried about that when it turned so cold last night. She said the fire would go out and her jars might burst.'

Mrs Peters' husband broke into a laugh.

'Well, can you beat the women! Held for murder, and worrying about her preserves!'

The young attorney set his lips.

'I guess before we're through with her she may have something more serious than preserves to worry about.'

'Oh, well,' said Mrs Hale's husband, with good-natured superiority, 'women are used to worrying over trifles.'

The two women moved a little closer together. Neither of them spoke. The county attorney seemed suddenly to remember his manners—and think of his future.

'And yet,' said he, with the gallantry of a young politician, 'for all their worries, what would we do without the ladies?'

The women did not speak, did not unbend. He went to the sink and began washing his hands. He turned to wipe them on the roller towel — whirled it for a cleaner place.

'Dirty towels! Not much of a housekeeper, would you say, ladies?'

He kicked his foot against some dirty pans under the sink.

'There's a great deal of work to be done on a farm' said Mrs Hale stiffly.

'To be sure. And yet'—with a little bow to her—'I know there are some Dickson County farm-houses that do not have such roller towels.' He gave it a pull to expose its full length again.

'Those towels get dirty awful quick. Men's hands aren't always as clean as they might be.'

'Ah, loyal to your sex, I see,' he laughed. He stopped and gave her a keen look. 'But you and Mrs Wright were neighbours. I suppose you were friends, too.'

Martha Hale shook her head.

'I've seen little enough of her of late years. I've not been in this house—in more than a year.'

'And why was that? You didn't like her?'

'I liked her well enough,' she replied with spirit. 'Farmers' wives have their hands full, Mr Henderson. And then'—she looked around the kitchen

'Yes?' he encouraged.

'It never seemed a very cheerful place,' said she, more to herself than to him.

'No,' he agreed; 'I don't think any one would call it cheerful. I shouldn't say she had the homemaking instinct.'

'Well, I don't know as Wright had, either,' she muttered.

'You mean they didn't get on very well?' he was quick to ask.

'No; I don't mean anything,' she answered, with decision. As she turned a little away from him she added: 'But I don't think a place would be any the cheerfuller for John Wright's bein' in it.'

'I'd like to talk to you about that a little later, Mrs Hale,' he said. 'I'm anxious to get the lay of things upstairs now.'

He moved toward the stair door, followed by the two men.

'I suppose anything Mrs Peters does'll be all right?' the sheriff inquired. 'She was to take in some clothes for her, you know—and a few little things. We left in such a hurry yesterday.'

The county attorney looked at the two women whom they were leaving alone there among the kitchen things.

'Yes—Mrs Peters,' he said, his glance resting on the woman who was not Mrs Peters, the big farmer woman who stood behind the sheriff's wife. 'Of course Mrs Peters is one of us,' he said, in a manner of entrusting responsibility. 'And keep your eye out, Mrs Peters, for anything that might be of use. No telling; you women might come upon a clue to the motive—and that's the thing we need.'

Mr Hale rubbed his face after the fashion of a show man getting ready for a pleasantry.

'But would the women know a clue if they did come upon it?' he said; and, having delivered himself of this, he followed the others through the stair door.

The women stood motionless and silent, listening to the footsteps, first upon the stairs, then in the room above them.

Then, as if releasing herself from something strange, Mrs Hale began to arrange the dirty pans under the sink, which the county attorney's disdainful push of the foot had deranged.

'I'd hate to have men comin' into my kitchen,' she said testily—'snoopin' round and criticisin'.'

'Of course it's no more than their duty,' said the sheriff's wife, in her manner of timid acquiescence.

'Duty's all right,' replied Mrs Hale bluffly, 'but I guess that deputy sheriff that come out to make the fire might have got a little of this on.' She gave the roller towel a pull. 'Wish I'd thought of that sooner! Seems mean to talk about her for not having things slicked up, when she had to come away in such a hurry.'

She looked around the kitchen. Certainly it was not "slicked up." Her eye was held by a bucket of sugar on a low shelf. The cover was off the wooden bucket, and beside it was a paper bag—half full.

Mrs Hale moved toward it.

'She was putting this in there', she said to herself—slowly.

She thought of the flour in her kitchen at home—half sifted, half not sifted. She had been interrupted, and had left things half done. What had interrupted Minnie Foster? Why had that work been left half done? She made a move as if to finish it,— unfinished things always bothered her,—and then she glanced around and saw that Mrs Peters was watching her— and she didn't want Mrs Peters to get that feeling she had got of work begun and then—for some reason—not finished.

'It's a shame about her fruit,' she said, and walked toward the cupboard that the county attorney had opened, and got on the chair, murmuring: 'I wonder if it's all gone.'

It was a sorry enough looking sight, but 'Here's one that's all right,' she said at last. She held it toward the light. 'This is cherries, too.' She looked again. 'I declare I believe that's the only one.'

With a sigh, she got down from the chair, went to the sink, and wiped off the bottle.

'She'll feel awful bad, after all her hard work in the hot weather. I remember the afternoon I put up my cherries last summer.'

She set the bottle on the table, and, with another sigh, started to sit down in the rocker. But she did not sit down. Something kept her from sitting down in that chair. She straightened—stepped back, and, half turned away, stood looking at it, seeing the woman who had sat there "pleatin' at her apron."

The thin voice of the sheriff's wife broke in upon her: 'I must be getting those things from the front room closet.' She opened the door into the other room, started in, stepped back. 'You coming with me, Mrs Hale?' she asked nervously. 'You— you could help me get them.'

They were soon back—the stark coldness of that shut-up room was not a thing to linger in.

'My!' said Mrs Peters, dropping the things on the table and hurrying to the stove.

Mrs Hale stood examining the clothes the woman who was being detained in town had said she wanted.

'Wright was close!' she exclaimed, holding up a shabby black skirt that bore the marks of much making over. 'I think maybe that's why she kept so much to herself. I s'pose she felt she couldn't do her part; and then, you don't enjoy things when you feel shabby. She used to wear pretty clothes and be lively—when she was Minnie Foster, one of the town girls, singing in the choir. But that—oh, that was twenty years ago.'

With a carefulness in which there was something tender, she folded the shabby clothes and piled them at one corner of the table. She looked up at Mrs Peters, and there was something in the other woman's look that irritated her.

'She don't care,' she said to herself. 'Much difference it makes to her whether Minnie Foster had pretty clothes when she was a girl.'

Then she looked again, and she wasn't so sure; in fact, she hadn't at any time been perfectly sure about Mrs Peters. She had that shrinking manner, and yet her eyes looked as if they could see a long way into things.

'This all you was to take in?' asked Mrs Hale.

'No,' said the sheriff's wife; 'she said she wanted an apron. Funny thing to want,' she ventured in her nervous little way, 'for there's not much to get you dirty in jail, goodness knows. But I suppose just to make her feel more natural. If you're used to wearing an apron—. She said they were in the bottom drawer of this cupboard. Yes—here they are. And then her little shawl that always hung on the stair door.'

She took the small grey shawl from behind the door leading upstairs, and stood a minute looking at it.

Suddenly Mrs Hale took a quick step toward the other woman.

'Mrs Peters!'

'Yes, Mrs Hale?'

'Do you think she—did it?'

A frightened look blurred the other things in Mrs Peters' eyes.

'Oh, I don't know,' she said, in a voice that seemed to shrink away from the subject.

'Well, I don't think she did,' affirmed Mrs Hale stoutly. 'Asking for an apron, and her little shawl. Worryin' about her fruit.'

'Mr Peters says—'Footsteps were heard in the room above; she stopped, looked up then went on in a lowered voice: 'Mr Peters says—it looks bad for her. Mr Henderson is awful sarcastic in a speech, and he's going to make fun of her saying she didn't—wake up.'

For a moment Mrs Hale had no answer. Then, 'Well, I guess John Wright didn't wake up—when they was slippin' that rope under his neck,' she muttered.

'No, it's *strange*,' breathed Mrs Peters. 'They think it was such a—funny way to kill a man.'

She began to laugh; at the sound of the laugh, abruptly stopped.

'That's just what Mr Hale said,' said Mrs Hale, in a resolutely natural voice. 'There was a gun in the house. He says that's what he can't understand.'

'Mr Henderson said, coming out, that what was needed for the case was a motive. Something to show anger—or sudden feeling.'

'Well, I don't see any signs of anger around here,' said Mrs Hale. 'I don't —'

She stopped. It was as if her mind tripped on something. Her eye was caught by a dish-towel in the middle of the kitchen table. Slowly she moved toward the table. One half of it was wiped clean, the other half messy. Her eyes made a slow, almost unwilling turn to the bucket of sugar and the half empty bag beside it. Things begun—and not finished.

After a moment she stepped back, and said, in that manner of releasing herself:

'Wonder how they're finding things upstairs? I hope she had it a little more flicked up up there. You know' she paused, and feeling gathered—'it seems kind of *sneaking*; locking her up in town and coming out here to get her own house to turn against her!'

'But, Mrs Hale,' said the sheriff's wife, 'the law is the law.'

'I s'pose 'tis,' answered Mrs Hale shortly.

She turned to the stove, saying something about that fire not being much to brag of. She worked with it a minute, and when she straightened up she said aggressively:

'The law is the law—and a bad stove is a bad stove. How'd you like to cook on this?'—pointing with the poker to the broken lining. She opened the oven door and started to express her opinion of the oven; but she was swept into her own thoughts, thinking of what it would mean, year after year, to have that stove to wrestle with. The thought of Minnie Foster trying to bake in that oven—and the thought of her never going over to see Minnie Foster—.

She was startled by hearing Mrs Peters say: 'A person gets discouraged—and loses heart.'

The sheriff's wife had looked from the stove to the sink—to the pail of water which had been carried in from outside. The two women stood there silent, above them the footsteps of the men who were looking for evidence against the woman who had worked in that kitchen. That look of seeing into things, of seeing through a thing to something else, was in the eyes of the sheriff's wife now. When Mrs Hale next spoke to her, it was gently:

'Better loosen up your things, Mrs Peters. We'll not feel them when we go out.'

Mrs Peters went to the back of the room to hang up the fur tippet she was wearing. A moment later she exclaimed, 'Why, she was piecing a quilt,' and held up a large sewing basket piled high with quilt pieces.

Mrs Hale spread some of the blocks on the table.

'It's log-cabin pattern,' she said, putting several of them together, 'Pretty, isn't it?'

They were so engaged with the quilt that they did not hear the footsteps on the stairs, just as the stair door opened Mrs Hale was saying:

'Do you suppose she was going to quilt it or just knot it?'

The sheriff threw up his hands.

'They wonder whether she was going to quilt it or just knot it!'

There was a laugh for the ways of women, a warming hands over the stove, and then the county attorney said briskly:

'Well, let's go right out to the barn and get that cleared up.'

'I don't see as there's anything so strange,' Mrs Hale said resentfully, after the outside door had closed on the three men —'our taking up our time with little things while we're waiting for them to get the evidence. I don't see as it's anything to laught about.'

'Of course they've got awful important things on their minds,' said the sheriff's wife apologetically.

They returned to an inspection of the block for the quilt. Mrs Hale was looking at the fine, even sewing, and preoccupied with thoughts of the woman who had done that sewing, when she heard the sheriff's wife say, in a queer tone:

'Why, look at this one.'

She turned to take the block held out to her.

'The sewing,' said Mrs Peters, in a troubled way. 'All the rest of them have been so nice and even—but—this one. Why, it looks as if she didn't know what she was about!'

Their eyes met—something flashed to life, passed between them, then, as if with an effort, they seemed to pull away from each other. A moment Mrs Hale sat there, her hands folded over that sewing which was so unlike all the rest of the sewing. Then she had pulled a knot and drawn the threads.

'Oh what are you doing, Mrs Hale?' asked the sheriff's wife, startled.

'Just pulling out a stitch or two that's not sewed very good,' said Mrs Hale mildly.

'I don't think we ought to touch things,' Mrs Peters said, a little helplessly.

'I'll just finish up this end,' answered Mrs Hale, still in that mild, matter-of-fact fashion.

She threaded a needle and started to replace bad sewing with good. For a little while she sewed in silence. Then, in that thin, timid voice, she heard:

'Mrs Hale!'

'Yes, Mrs Peters?'

'What do you suppose she was so—nervous about?'

'Oh, *I* don't know,' said Mrs Hale, as if dismissing a thing not important enough to spend much time on. 'I don't know as she was—nervous. I sew awful queer sometimes when I'm just tired.'

She cut a thread, and out of the corner of her eye looked up at Mrs Peters. The small, lean face of the sheriff's wife seemed to have tightened up. Her eyes had that look of peering into something. But the next moment she moved, and said in her thin, indecisive way.

'Well, I must get those clothes wrapped. They may be through sooner than we think. I wonder where I could find a piece of paper—and string.'

'In that cupboard, maybe,' suggested Mrs Hale, after a glance around.

One piece of the crazy sewing remained unripped. Mrs Peters' back turned, Martha Hale now scrutinised that piece, compared it with the dainty, accurate sewing of the other blocks. The difference was startling. Holding this block made her feel queer, as if the distracted thoughts of the woman who had perhaps turned to it to try and quiet herself were communicating themselves to her.

Mrs Peter's voice roused her.

'Here's a bird-cage,' she said. 'Did she have a bird, Mrs Hale?'

'Why, I don't know whether she did or not.' She turned to look at the cage Mrs Peters was holding up, 'I've not been here in so long.' She sighed. 'There was a man round last year selling canaries cheap—but I don't know as she took one. Maybe she did. She used to sing real pretty herself.'

Mrs Peters looked around the kitchen.

'Seems kind of funny to think of a bird here.' She half laughed—an attempt to put up a barrier. 'But she must have had one—or why would she have a cage? I wonder what happened to it.'

'I suppose maybe the cat got it,' suggested Mrs Hale, resuming her sewing.

'No; she didn't have a cat. She's got that feeling some people have about cats—being afraid of them. When they brought her to our house yesterday, my cat got in the room, and she was real upset and asked me to take it out.'

'My sister Bessie was like that,' laughed Mrs Hale.

The sheriff's wife did not reply. The silence made Mrs Hale turn round. Mrs Peters was examining the bird-cage.

'Look at this door,' she said slowly. 'It's broke. One hinge has been pulled apart.'

Mrs Hale came nearer.

'Looks as if some one must have been—rough with it.'

Again their eyes met—startled, questioning, apprehensive. For a moment neither spoke nor stirred. Then Mrs Hale, turning away, said brusquely:

'If they're going to find any evidence, I wish they'd be about it. I don't like this place.'

'But I'm awful glad you came with me, Mrs Hale.' Mrs Peters put the bird-cage on the table and sat down. 'It would be lonesome for me—sitting here alone.'

'Yes, it would, wouldn't it?' agreed Mrs Hale, a certain determined naturalness in her voice. She had picked up the sewing, but now it dropped in her lap, and she murmured in a different voice: 'But I tell you what I *do* wish, Mrs Peters. I wish I had come over sometimes when she was here. I wish—I had.'

'But of course you were awful busy, Mrs Hale. Your house—and your children.'

'I could've come,' retorted Mrs Hale shortly. 'I stayed away because it weren't cheerful—and that's why I ought to have come. I'—she looked around—'I've never liked this place. Maybe because it's down in a hollow and you don't see the road. I don't know what it is, but it's a lonesome place, and always was. I wish I had come over to see Minnie Foster sometimes. I can see now—.' She did not put it into words.

'Well, you mustn't reproach yourself,' counselled Mrs Peters. 'Somehow, we just don't see how it is with other folks till— something comes up.'

'Not having children makes less work,' mused Mrs Hale, after a silence, 'but it makes a quiet house—and Wright out to work all day—and no company when he did come in. Did you know John Wright, Mrs Peters?'

'Not to know him. I've seen him in town. They say he was a good man.'

'Yes—good,' conceded John Wright's neighbour grimly. 'He didn't drink, and kept his word as well as most, I guess, and paid his debts. But he was a hard man, Mrs Peters. Just to pass the time of day with him—.' She stopped, shivered a little. 'Like a raw wind that gets to the bone.' Her eye fell upon the cage on the table before her, and she added, almost bitterly: 'I should think she would've wanted a bird!'

Suddenly she leaned forward, looking intently at the cage. 'But what do you s'pose went wrong with it?'

'I don't know,' returned Mrs Peters; 'unless it got sick and died.'

But after she said it she reached over and swung the broken door. Both women watched it as if somehow held by it.

'You didn't know—her?' Mrs Hale asked, a gentler note in her voice.

'Not till they brought her yesterday,' said the sheriff's wife.

'She—come to think of it, she was kind of like a bird herself. Real sweet and pretty, but kind of timid and—fluttery. How — she—did—change.'

That held her for a long time. Finally, as if struck with a happy thought and relieved to get back to everyday things, she exclaimed:

'Tell you what, Mrs Peters, why don't you take the quilt in with you? It might take up her mind.'

'Why, I think that's a real nice idea, Mrs Hale,' agreed the sheriff's wife, as if she too were glad to come into the atmosphere of a simple kindness. 'There couldn't possibly be any objection to that, could there? Now, just what will I take? I wonder if her patches are in here—and her things.'

They turned to the sewing basket.

'Here's some red,' said Mrs Hale, bringing out a roll of cloth. Underneath that was a box. 'Here, maybe her scissors are in here—and her things.' She held it up. 'What a pretty box! I'll warrant that was something she had a long time ago—when she was a girl.'

She held it in her hand a moment; then, with a little sigh, opened it.

Instantly her hand went to her nose.

'Why—!'

Mrs Peters drew nearer—then turned away.

'There's something wrapped up in this piece of silk,' faltered Mrs Hale.

'This isn't her scissors,' said Mrs Peters, in a shrinking voice.

Her hand not steady, Mrs Hale raised the piece of silk. 'Oh, Mrs Peters!' she cried. 'It's—'

Mrs Peters bent closer.

'It's the bird,' she whispered.

'But, Mrs Peters!' cried Mrs Hale. '*Look* at it! Its neck—look at its neck—It's all—other side *to*.'

She held the box away from her.

The sheriff's wife again bent closer.

'Somebody wrung its neck,' said she, in a voice that was slow and deep.

And then again the eyes of the two women met—this time clung together in a look of dawning comprehension, of growing horror. Mrs Peters looked from the dead bird to the broken door of the cage. Again their eyes met. And just then there was a sound at the outside door.

Mrs Hale slipped the box under the quilt pieces in the basket, and sank into the chair before it. Mrs Peters stood holding to the table. The county attorney and the sheriff came in from outside.

'Well, ladies,' said the county attorney, as one turning from serious things to little pleasantries, 'have you decided whether she was going to quilt it or knot it?'

'We think,' began the sheriff's wife in a flurried voice, 'that she was going to—knot it.'

He was too preoccupied to notice the change that came in her voice on that last.

'Well, that's very interesting, I'm sure,' he said tolerantly. He caught sight of the bird-cage. 'Has the bird flown?'

'We think the cat got it,' said Mrs Hale in a voice curiously even.

He was walking up and down, as if thinking something out.

'Is there a cat?' he asked absently.

Mrs Hale shot a look up at the sheriff's wife.

'Well, not *now*,' said Mrs Peters. 'They're superstitious, you know; they leave.'

She sank into her chair.

The county attorney did not heed her. 'No sign at all of any one having come in from outside,' he said to Peters, in the manner of continuing an interrupted conversation. 'Their own rope. Now let's go upstairs again and go over it, piece by piece. It would have to have been some one who knew just the—'

The stair door closed behind them and their voices were lost.

The two women sat motionless, not looking at each other, but as if peering into something and at the same time holding back. When they spoke now it was as if they were afraid of what they were saying, but as if they could not help saying it.

'She liked the bird,' said Martha Hale, low and slowly. 'She was going to bury it in that pretty box.'

'When I was a girl,' said Mrs Peters, under her breath, 'my kitten—there was a boy took a hatchet, and before my eyes—before I could get there—' She covered her face an instant. 'If they hadn't held me back I would have'—she caught herself, looked upstairs where footsteps were heard, and finished weakly—'hurt him.'

Then they sat without speaking or moving.

'I wonder how it would seem,' Mrs Hale at last began, as if feeling her way over strange ground—'never to have had any children around?' Her eyes made a slow sweep of the kitchen, as if seeing what that kitchen had meant through all the years. 'No, Wright wouldn't like the bird,' she said after that—'a thing that sang. She used to sing. He killed that too.' Her voice tightened.

Mrs Peters moved uneasily.

'Of course we don't know who killed the bird.'

'I knew John Wright,' was Mrs Hale's answer.

'It was an awful thing was done in this house that night, Mrs Hale,' said the sheriff's wife. 'Killing a man while he slept—slipping a thing round his neck that choked the life out of him.'

Mrs Hale's hand went out to the bird-cage.

'His neck. Choked the life out of him.'

'We don't *know* who killed him,' whispered Mrs Peters wildly. 'We don't *know*.'

Mrs Hale had not moved. 'If there had been years and years of—nothing, then a bird to sing to you, it would be awful—still—after the bird was still.'

It was as if something within her not herself had spoken, and it found in Mrs Peters something she did not know as herself.

'I know what stillness is,' she said, in a queer, monotonous voice. 'When we homesteaded in Dakota, and my first baby died—after he was two years old—and me with no other then—'

Mrs Hale stirred.

'How soon do you suppose they'll be through looking for the evidence?'

'I know what stillness is,' repeated Mrs Peters, in just that same way. Then she too pulled back. 'The law has got to punish crime, Mrs Hale,' she said in her tight little way.

'I wish you'd seen Minnie Foster,' was the answer, 'when she wore a white dress with blue ribbons, and stood up there in the choir and sang.'

The picture of that girl, the fact that she had lived neighbour to that girl for twenty years, and had let her die for lack of life, was suddenly more than she could bear.

'Oh, I *wish* I'd come over here once in a while!' she cried. 'That was a crime! That was a crime! Who's going to punish that?'

'We mustn't take on,' said Mrs Peters, with a frightened look toward the stairs.

'I might 'a' *known* she needed help! I tell you, it's *queer*, Mrs Peters. We live close together, and we live far apart. We all go through the same things—it's all just a different kind of the same thing! If it weren't—why do you and I *understand*? Why do we *know*–what we know this minute?'

She dashed her hand across her eyes. Then, seeing the jar of fruit on the table, she reached for it and choked out:

'If I was you I wouldn't *tell* her her fruit was gone! Tell her it *ain't*. Tell her it's all right—all of it. Here—take this in to prove it to her! She—she may never know whether it was broke or not.'

She turned away.

Mrs Peters reached out for the bottle of fruit as if she were glad to take it—as if touching a familiar thing, having something to do, could keep her from something else. She got up, looked about for something to wrap the fruit in, took a petticoat from the pile of clothes she had brought from the front room, and nervously started winding that round the bottle.

'My!' she began, in a high, false voice, 'it's a good thing the men couldn't hear us! Getting all stirred up over a little thing like a—dead canary.' She hurried over that. 'As if that could have anything to do with—with—My, wouldn't they *laugh*?'

Footsteps were heard on the stairs.

'Maybe they would,' muttered Mrs Hale—'maybe they wouldn't'

'No, Peters,' said the county attorney incisively: 'it's all perfectly clear, except the reason for doing it. But you know juries when it comes to women. If there was some definite thing—something to show. Something to make a story about. A thing that would connect up with this clumsy way of doing it.'

In a covert way Mrs Hale looked at Mrs Peters. Mrs Peters was looking at her. Quickly they looked away from each other. The outer door opened and Mr Hale came in.

'I've got the team round now,' he said. 'Pretty cold out there.'

'I'm going to stay here awhile by myself,' the county attorney suddenly announced. 'You can send Frank out for me, can't you?' he asked the sheriff. 'I want to go over everything. I'm not satisfied we can't do better.'

Again, for one brief moment, the two women's eyes found one another.

The sheriff came up to the table.

'Did you want to see what Mrs Peters was going to take in?'

The county attorney picked up the apron. He laughed.

'Oh, I guess they're not very dangerous things the ladies have picked out.'

Mrs Hale's hand was on the sewing basket in which the box was concealed. She felt that she ought to take her hand off the basket. She did not seem able to. He picked up one of the quilt blocks which she had piled on to cover the box. Her eyes felt like fire. She had a feeling that if he took up the basket she would snatch it from him.

But he did not take it up. With another little laugh, he turned away, saying:

'No; Mrs Peters doesn't need supervising. For that matter, a sheriff's wife is married to the law. Ever think of it that way, Mrs Peters?'

Mrs Peters was standing beside the table. Mrs Hale shot a look up at her; but she could not see her face. Mrs Peters had turned away. When she spoke, her voice was muffled.

'Not—just that way,' she said.

'Married to the law!' chuckled Mrs Peters' husband. He moved toward the door into the front room, and said to the county attorney:

'I just want you to come in here a minute, George. We ought to take a look at these windows.'

'Oh—windows,' said the county attorney scoffingly.

'We'll be right out, Mr Hale,' said the sheriff to the farmer, who was still waiting by the door.

Hale went to look after the horses. The sheriff followed the county attorney into the other room. Again—for one final moment—the two women were alone in that kitchen.

Martha Hale sprang up, her hands tight together, looking at that other woman, with whom it rested. At first she could not see her eyes, for the sheriff's wife had not turned back since she turned away at that suggestion of being married to the law. But now Mrs Hale made her turn back. Her eyes made her turn back. Slowly, unwillingly, Mrs Peters turned her head until her eyes met the eyes of the other woman. There was a moment when they held each other in a steady, burning look in which there was no evasion nor flinching. Then Martha Hale's eyes pointed the way to the basket in which was hidden the thing that would make certain the conviction of the other woman—that woman who was not there and yet who had been there with them all through that hour.

For a moment Mrs Peters did not move. And then she did it. With a rush forward, she threw back the quilt pieces, got the box, tried to put it in her handbag. It was too big. Desperately she opened it, started to take the bird out. But there she broke—she could not touch the bird. She stood there helpless, foolish.

There was the sound of a knob turning in the inner door. Martha Hale snatched the box from the sheriff's wife, and got it in the pocket of her big coat just as the sheriff and the county attorney came back into the kitchen.

'Well, Henry,' said the county attorney facetiously, 'at least we found out that she was not going to quilt it. She was going to—what is it you call it, ladies?'

Mrs Hale's hand was against the pocket of her coat.

'We call it—knot it, Mr Henderson.'

ILA ARAB MEHTA

S*moke*

Ba comes back this evening by the five o'clock train. Shubha glanced at her watch. It was only four o'clock, still some time to go. A vast sea of overpowering emptiness engulfed her being. Nothing left to do. Nothing ...except wait.

Her hands wandered over the books lying on the table and picked one up. It was a fat book written in English on women's health problems and their treatment. It opened with the picture of a naked woman, bared in vivid detail, sketched with dexterity. For clinical purposes only, of course!

She slammed it shut, pushed it back and walked out of the room on to the open balcony. She stood still. The oppressive tormenting afternoon was still astride the earth, its heat permeating every nook and cranny. 'Like my own emptiness,' she thought. 'Not a hollow neutral vacuum but this leaden emptiness, opaque and solid.

'The russet evening shall wax but a few moments only. And then all will be dark again.' A wan smile on her lips, Shubha stepped back into the room.

Just half-past four. Driving her car towards the station, Dr Shubha scolded herself, 'You're becoming neurotic, Shubha. The sun itself looks like a dark blot to you.'

Suddenly her belly tighened. Was everything ship-shape for Ba's homecoming? All details seen to? Like unwinding the reel of a film, she went over the house slowly, room by room, in her mind's eye. Nothing amiss. All in order. Each corner had been cleaned with care. But suppose...? Well—her practice and the clinic really left her with no time to spare. Her mother-in-law knew it well. And those few snatched private moments, well, forget it. It's just as well Ba did not get to know.

Swiftly, suddenly, a cold shiver rose from the pit of her stomach to her throat, with a chilling reminder—the picture! The photograph of Subodh had been left undusted, with the dirty grey string of dried flowers hanging around it. She had forgotten to place a fresh wreath. And with it remained Bapuji's photograph too. Ba would of course go straight up to them, first thing on coming home.

Framed in dry dead petals, Subodh's face smiled unmoving in black and white—like the printed picture of Krishna on last year's Diwali card, chucked on top of a heap of discarded papers.

Shubha gripped the steering wheel hard.

The ashtray beside the telephone—had it been cleaned? Often, ever so often, in these past few days she had sat there smoking as she talked over the telephone. Suppose Ba were to ask why we needed an ashtray at all in our house? What then? Oh God! There was no time now to turn back to house. She parked the car and went into the station.

The train arrived on time. The luggage was stacked into the car. Shubha slid behind the wheel and started the engine and Ba got in beside her. Inching her way through milling crowds, sounding the horn intermittently, slamming the brakes on at traffic lights, she drove homeward. The driving, the traffic and the tortuous progress, she had grown used to it all by now and could manage mechanically.

Ba talked. As she talked, the fatigue of the journey was shot through with the lively satisfaction that lit her face. Crisply, rapidly, Ba went about recounting the little happenings and family gossip, as she always did. Like the clickety-clack of needles knitting all the inconsequential details into the common tale of the extended Indian family. Aunt, nephew, cousin, grandmother, criss-crossing relatives gathered together to celebrate or to mourn.

The car ran on. For it had to run on. Ba's words flitted out of the window like dry leaves swept along by the afternoon breeze. Shubha was quiet. Her thoughts hovered round that ashtray near the telephone—cigarette ash wafting in the air.

Home at last. Pressing the horn twice to summon a servant, Shubha ran up the stairs, not even waiting for Ba to alight. She went straight to the telephone. No ashtray there. Damn it! She herself had put it away into the cupboard this morning.

Ba came up and headed straight for the photographs. Bapuji and Subodh smiled through the film of dust. Only four months after Shubha had stepped in as a bride, father and son had died together in a road accident.

A crystal bowl decked with fresh young blossoms had dashed to the floor and shattered. Since then, like the myriad splinters of glass, were the moments of life, each to be picked up, one at a time, and one by one to be put away.

Ba carefully cleaned the photographs, knelt down and touched her head to the floor. Rising she turned to Shubha, and on a faintly reproachful note asked, 'My dear, how did so much dust gather? Surely you remembered the fresh flowers and obeisance every day?'

One could make excuses—of a patient being ill, of visits to be paid. But words failed Shubha. She walked out of the room slowly.

Outside, she stood leaning against the rails of the balcony. Ba, she thought, must now be busy washing and bathing. At once she was seized with an irrepressible urge. The small space between thumb and finger throbbed palpably.

She went back to the room. Ba would take a long time in her bath. She pulled the packet out with an impatient hand and lit a cigarette, taking in the first few drags hungrily. Oh God. Just to quell the restless thirst of hours...

One cigarette smoked, she lit another from its end. This too must be finished before Ba came out. She stood there and inhaled the smoke, deep and steady.

But how long can this go on? How long can the act be kept secret from her mother-in-law? There was the clinic, of course, where she could smoke. But Ba might just walk in there too, one day.

The sound of the bathroom door being unlatched broke her

reverie. She flung the cigarette away, turned her head and peered. No, Ba was not yet back. She drew a long breath and sank down on the cane sofa.

Life. How it stretched, interminably. How inexorably the seconds tick away. No might in the world can give them a shove and push them back. Time...

A wave of exhaustion swept over her all at once. As if she had been plodding miles, carrying a heavy load. Now she only wanted to sit, just sit with a cigarette dangling from her listless hand.

'Don't you have to go to the clinic today?' Ba's voice reached out to her.

I'm going,' she answered and snapped her purse shut. But she remained rooted to the sofa. The prospect of the clinic was depressing.

The faces that waited for her there would be dismal, every one of them, some bereft of all hope. To think of them was to enter that grey realm. 'I cannot eat a morsel, doctor.' 'A fever of 100° since yesterday.' 'The swellings on the feet have not gone down.' Some throats riddled with swollen glands, some tumours destined to live or to die, a ceaseless tug-of-war and unending complaints.

She heaved a sigh and just as she was about to rise and leave, Ba came in. Seeing Shubha still sitting, she drew up the cane chair opposite and sat down.

'Shubha, the wedding was really great fun, very enjoyable. Oh dear, we—now let's see, how many years since I last saw a wedding? Your wedding, of course, and after that—oh well. But Mama was hurt that you did not attend. I explained to him of course. She is a doctor, I said. She has a commitment to her patients. Far be it from me to come in the way of her duty. What do you say? Isn't that so?

An answer. One must say something now. Ba was waiting for a response. That is how it should be—some give and take, some conversation. Without these mundane exchanges, a home would freeze into one of those two dimensional stills. Her voice, pitched a shade too high, broke the lengthening pause. 'How did Indu look as a bride? Was she dressed heavily for the occasion?'

'Yes indeed, dear. They had called in one of these make-up artistes, you know. A full hundred rupees she charged! But Indu looked like a doll.'

Ba pulled herself up a bit and continued, 'You know Shubha, it really makes me laugh. These modern girls are all just like dolls, mere dolls. Not a jot of idealism, noble thoughts or sensibilities.'

Shubha gazed out in silence as the evening spread its shadow over the earth. She looked into the falling darkness.

'Come, now. You'll be late for work,' Ba said.

She rose to her feet. Clutching the balustrade firmly in hand, she walked down the steps and out of the house. She started the car but after a moment switched off the engine. She would walk to the clinic today, she decided. It was a short distance only and she was in no mood to drive.

At the clinic, she found a large number of patients waiting for her. She took them all in at a glance. At the end of the line sat a man, neatly dressed, middle-aged. Their eyes met. An enigmatic smile played on his lips as he said, 'Have been waiting for you ever so long.'

Shubha reacted with a start. It was not the words or voice so much, but the smile that was disquieting. A shiver of fear. As if this man could read her mind, as if he knew all, inside out.

She turned her eyes away in haste. She sat erect in her chair and answered, a trifle too loudly, a trifle too crisply. 'Sorry, I have been delayed a bit.'

One after another the patients came up to her. Some were advised to consult a specialist—for some an X-ray, for others merely an aspirin. It was all so routine. And the eyes of the man at the end of the queue somehow radiated strength to her—enhancing her capabilities, her insight, and her confidence. Yet there was that under-current of irritability, a weariness, an overwhelming desire just to let go ...!

She glanced at him. His smile hurt her, chased her about like some little whirligig, a sparkler that children light on festival nights which scatters a shower of thrill and fear round and round in its zig-zag trail.

Most of the patients had departed. It was his turn now—the last one. A cigarette. The urgent need to smoke welled up in her. Her fingers pulled out a cigarette from her purse. The man sprung up and lit it with his own lighter.

'Thank you.'

He then sat down in the chair opposite her.

'Latika has been unwell since yesterday. Doctor, would you please come?'

His voice now struck dread, like his haunting smile. His words, so mildly spoken, were a confident invitation. Beneath the words lay the phrases unspoken: 'I know ... I know it all ... everything.'

She stood up and said, 'Yes, let's go. We shall watch for a day or two and then maybe call in a specialist.'

He picked up Shubha's black bag, walked ahead to his car and held the door open for her. A moments pause, then Shubha got into the front seat. He closed the door with care, walked round and got in beside her, behind the wheel.

Latika was of course not yet as well as she ought to be, but even so her condition did not quite merit a house call. Still, Shubha spent a long evening at their house. Long-ailing spinster and her bachelor brother together managed to keep the evening scintillating. She sat for a long time with the brother and sister, savouring the easy flow of conversation. The simple chatter that bounces off the walls of a house giving it the dimensions of a home. The fear of that smile had now vanished. Skeins of laughter and companionship spun a shimmering cocoon around her.

'Doctor, stay back and eat with us,' begged Latika. Shubha sprang up with a start and looked at her watch. Nine-thirty! Ba waited at home for her. She had returned ...

'No thank you—it's late. Some other time.' She stood up.

'I had no idea of your taste in these things. I have a number of imported brands—cigarettes as well as drinks,' he said.

'Oh, no! It's only occassional...' Murmuring, she crossed to the telephone, called the clinic, told the compounder to close for the day. She felt agitated, scared. She had lingered too long—the laughter, the jokes—for no good reason on earth. Life. She felt alive, and yet dreaded the very touch of life, afraid to come alive.

He drove her home in his car. Lifting her black bag in his

hand, he offered to carry it upstairs. But she took it from him with a 'No, thank you.'

He did not move but looked at her and said softly, 'Will you not come again, unless my sister is ill? Won't you come over just to see us? We have really enjoyed your visit. You see, we are quite alone.'

She could no longer stand there. Mumbling a formal 'Yes, of course' she quickly climbed the steps.

A cloud of sweet incense hit her at the door. She entered the living room and saw the two photographs of Subodh and Bapuji draped with thick garlands of flowers. A bunch of incense sticks burned before them. The air hung heavy with the sweet scent. Ba sat on the floor facing the pictures, reciting the Gita.

Softly, Subha crossed over to her room, put down her purse and taking the cigarette packet out, tucked it away into the cupboard. She washed her hands and face and rinsed her mouth with antiseptic. When she returned to the living room Ba had finished her recitation and was spooning the food onto the plates.

'I had to call on a patient. It got late,' she said and sat down to eat.

Ba's hand stopped still in mid-air. Shubha jumped up and prostrated herself before Subodh's photograph. Subodh was smiling at her—a distant lifeless smile framed by fresh voluptuous blossoms.

As they ate, Ba began to talk again. Shubha barely heard her. Her thoughts, her being were still in Latika's house. The faint whiff of after-shave lotion, light laughter. 'You see, we are quite alone.' His words, his eyes...

'We are quite alone.' She heard the words distinctly again and looked up, startled. It was Ba talking to her.

'I told your Mama , "Do not worry for us, brother, what if we are quite alone? I and my dear Shubha, we are quite apart from others".'

Shubha looked down at her plate as she ate. Ba spoke on.

'Mama was all too full of praise, dear. "Shubha is indeed a saint," he said. "Her life is like an incense stick. It burns itself to release its fragrance into the world".'

Suddenly, Ba's voice ceased. Shubha looked up at her mother-in-law. A deep frown knitting her brow, Ba stared steadily into the corner opposite. She got up and walked over, and picked up something from the floor.

'Shubha, what is this?' Ba's voice cracked. Like hard dry earth. The barren sunbaked earth cracks, willy-nilly, along deep jagged fissures.

With thin trembling fingers Ba held up the burnt-out stub of a cigarette.

The Picture

Amal's eyes came to rest on the spray that left behind it, against the horizon, a zigzag thread of sunrays in the colours of the rainbow: a marvellous spectrum which could scarcely be seen unless one tilted one's head at a particular angle and looked hard. She pointed it out to her husband facing her across the table in the Casino overlooking the meeting-place of the sea and Nile at Ras al-Barr. He could not see it. If only he could have. The spectrum disappears when it's really there, then one imagines it to be there when in fact it has disappeared with the waves rolling away from the rocks of the promontory known as *The Tongue* which juts out at this spot. The waves of the sea start butting against the rock once more and the spray resumes its upward surge.

'There it is, Izzat,' Amal shouted in excitement, and her son Midhat grasped the hem of her dress and followed her gaze.

'Where?—Mummy—where?' he said in disjointed words that didn't ripen into a sentence.

The look of boredom faded from Izzat's eyes and he burst out laughing. An effendi, wearing a tarboosh and suit complete with waistcoat, shouted: 'Double five, my dear sir, double five,' and rapped the board with the backgammon pieces, at which the fat man swallowed his spittle and pulled aside the front of his fine white damascene *galabia** to mop away the sweat. An old photographer wearing a black suit jogged his young assistant, who was taking a nap leaning against the developing bucket. The seller of tombola tickets, brushing the sand from his bare feet, called out: 'Couldn't *you* be the lucky one?' Amal gave her shy, apologetic smile and then she was overcome by infectious laughter so that she burst out laughing without knowing why. Suddenly she stopped as she realised she was happy.

'Daddy—food—Mummy—ice cream!'

Izzat turned round in search of the waiter. His gaze became riveted to the Casino entrance and he smiled, turning down his thick, moist lower lip. His hand streched out mechanically and undid another of the buttons of his white shirt, revealing a wider expanse of thick hair on his chest.

The table behind Amal was taken over by a woman of about thirty who was wearing shorts that exposed her white rounded thighs, while her blonde dyed hair was tied round with a red georgette handkerchief decorated with white jasmine, and another woman of about fifty the front of whose dress revealed a brown expanse of wrinkled bosom. Izzat clapped his hands energetically for the waiter who was actually close enough to have come at a mere sign.

'Three—three ice creams!'

Amal was horrified at her husband's sudden extravagance. 'Two's enough, Izzat,' she whispered, her face flushed. 'I don't really want one.'

Izzat gave no sign of having heard her. He kept repeating, 'Three ices—ice creams—mixed—got it?' in an excited voice.

When the waiter moved away, Izzat called him back again and again and said, stressing every syllable:

'Make one of them vanilla. Yes, vanilla. Vanilla ice cream!'

Amal relaxed, smiling triumphantly. 'Where is it all coming from?' her mother had asked her. 'Surely not from the fifteen pounds a month he earns? Have you been saving? No wonder, poor thing, your hands are all cracked with washing and you're nothing but skin and bone. What a shame he doesn't

**galabia*: headcovering

understand and appreciate you properly. He's leading you a dog's life while he gallivants around.'

Amal pursed her lips derisively. She and Izzat together, at last, really on holiday at a hotel in Ras al-Barr! A fortnight without cooking or washing or polishing, no more waiting up for him, no more of that sweltering heat. She bent her head back proudly as she swept back a lock of jet black hair from her light brown forehead. She caught sight of Izzat's eyes and felt her throat constrict: once again the fire was in those eyes that had become as though sightless, that hovered over things but never settled on them. He had begun to see, his eyes sparkling anew with that fire that was both captivating and submissive, which both burned and pleaded. That glance of his! She had forgotten it—or had she set out intentionally to forget so that she would not miss it? The fact was that it had come back and it was as if he had never been without it. Was it the summer resort? Was it being on holiday? Anyway it was enveloping her once again in a fever of heat.

Amal noticed Izzat's dark brown hand with its swollen veins and she was swept by an ungovernable longing to bend over and kiss it. The tears welled in her eyes and she drew Midhat close to her with fumbling hands and covered him with kisses from cheek to ear, hugging him to her, and when the moment of frenzy that had stormed her body died down she released him and began searching for the spectrum of colours through her tears as she inclined her head to one side. She must not be misled: was that really the spectrum, or just a spectrum produced by her tears?... 'Tomorrow you'll weep blood instead of tears,' her mother had told her, and her father had said: 'You're young, my child, and tomorrow love and all that rubbish will be over and only the drudgery will be left.' Amal shook her head as though driving away a fly that had landed on her cheek and murmured to herself: 'You don't understand at all...I...I've found the one thing I've been looking for all my life.' Her eyes caught the spectrum and she awoke to a metallic jarring sound as the glass of ice cream scraped against the marble table.

'Three ice creams, two mixed and one vanilla.'

'I'll look after the vanilla, old chap. Vanilla will do me fine,' said Izzat, carefully enunciating his words and giving a significant smile in the direction of—which direction? A suggestive female laugh came back in reply. In reply to the smile? Amal cupped the iced glass in her hands and turned round as she watched him. White—vanilla—strawberry—pistachio— and the yellow ice? Would it be mango or apricot? Colouring, mere colouring. It can't be—it can't be.

'Why don't you eat it?' asked Izzat.

She took up the spoon and was about to scoop the ice cream when she put it down and again cradled the glass in her hand.

Izzat spoke to his son.

'Ice cream tasty, Midhat?'

'Tasty!'

'As tasty as you, my little darling.'

A second laugh rang out behind Amal. Her hands tightened round the iced glass from which cold, icy steam was rising, like smoke. She raised her eyes and reluctantly turned her head without moving her shoulder, slowly lest someone see her, afraid of what she might see. She saw her, *white as a wall, a cradle, white as vanilla ice*. For a fleeting moment her eyes met those of the white-skinned woman in the shorts. Her lower lip trembled and she looked back at her glass, drawing herself up. She sat there stiffly, eating. The woman in the shorts took a cigarette from her handbag and left it dangling from her lips until the woman with the bare expanse of bosom had lit it for her. She began to puff out smoke provocatively in Amal's direction, but Amal did not look at her any more. She was a loose woman. Izzat hardly said a word without her laughing. Obviously a loose woman and he wasn't to blame.

Midhat finished his ice cream and began glancing around him listlessly, his lips pursed as though he was about to cry.

'*The Tongue*, I want to go to *The Tongue*.'

Amal sighed with relief: a great worry had been removed. This loose woman would be removed from her sight for ever more. She bent her head to one side, smiled, and said carefully as though playing a part before an audience.

'Certainly, darling. Now. Right now Daddy and Mummy'll take Midhat and go to *The Tongue*.'

She pushed back her chair as she gave a short affected laugh.

'Where to?' said Izzat with unwarranted gruffness.

'The child wants to go to *The Tongue*.'

'And where are we going after *The Tongue?* Surely we're not going to suffocate ourselves back at the hotel so early?'

Midhat burst out crying, trammelling the ground with his feet. Amal jumped up, clasping the child to her nervously. *Izzat? Izzat wants to—it's not possible—good God, it's not possible*—Midhat, irked by the violence with which he was being held, intensified his howling.

'Shut up!' Izzat shouted at him.

When Midhat didn't stop, his father jumped up and seized him from his mother's arms, giving him two quick slaps on the hand. Then Izzat sat down again and said, as though justifying himself:

'I won't have a child who's a cry-baby!'

Amal returned to her chair, and the tears ran silently from Midhat's eyes and down to the corners of his mouth. As though she had just woken up, the woman in the shorts said in her drawling husky voice:

'Come along, my sweetheart. Come along to me.' She took a piece of chocolate wrapped in red paper out of her pocket.

'Come, my darling! Come and take the chocolate!'

Amal drew Midhat to her. The woman in the shorts put her head to one side and crossed her legs. Smiling slightly, she threw the piece of chocolate on to the table so that Midhat could see it. Amal cradled Midhat's head against her breast, patting his hair with trembling hands. Midhat lay quietly against his mother's breast for a while; then he lifted an arm to wipe away the tears, and, peeping from under his arm, he began to steal fleeting glances at the chocolate. The woman in the shorts beckoned and winked at him, and Amal buried his head in her breast. *It's not possible, not possible that he would go to her—Izzat—Midhat—it's not possible that Izzat would want her.* With a sudden movement Midhat disengaged himself from his mother's grasp and ran to the neighbouring table. The lewd laugh rang out anew, long and jarring.

'Go and fetch the boy!' Amal whispered, her lips blue.

Izzat smiled defiantly. 'Fetch him yourself!'

'We're not beggars,' she said in a choked voice.

'Where does the begging come in to it? Or do you want the

boy to turn out as timid as you?'

Amal didn't look at the table behind where her son sat on the lap of the woman in shorts eating chocolate and getting it all over his mouth and chin, hands and shirt. She wished that she could take him and beat him till he—but what had he done wrong? The fault was hers, hers alone.

'Good for us; we've finished the chocolate and now—up we get and wash our hands,' the woman in shorts drawled in her husky voice.

Amal jumped to her feet, white-faced. The woman in the shorts went off, waggling her hips as she dragged Midhat along behind her.

Putting a hand on his wife's shoulder, Izzat said softly:

'You stay here while I go and fetch the boy.'

Amal remained standing, watching the two of them: the woman with Midhat holding her hand, the woman and Izzat following her. She watched them as they crossed the balcony of the Casino and—through glass—as they crossed the inner lounge and were lost behind the walls of the building, the woman's buttocks swaying as though detached from her, with Izzat following her, his body tilted forward as though about to pounce. For step after step, step hard upon step, lewd step upon lewd step. 'No, Izzat, don't be like that. You frighten me, you frighten me when you're like that, Izzat.' She had spoken these words as she dropped down exhausted on a rock in the grotto at the Aquarium. Izzat had been out of breath as he said: 'You can't imagine—you can't imagine how much I love you, Amal,' with pursed lips and half-closed eyes, heavy with the look of a cat calling its mate, a look that burned and pleaded. *Izzat and the other woman—and the same look that burned and pleaded...It can't be—It can't be.*

'A picture, Madam?'

Amal had collapsed exhausted on the chair, waving the old photographer away. 'No, Izzat—no, don't put your hand on my neck like that! What'll people say when they see the photo? They'll say I'm in love with you—No please don't.' 'Here you are, Milady, the picture's been taken with my hand on your neck and now you'll never be able to get rid of me.'

'A postcard size for ten piastres and no waiting, Madam.' ·

'Not now, not now.'

The man went on his way repeating in a listless, lilting voice, 'family pictures, souvenir pictures,' while behind him the barefooted tombola ticket-seller wiped his hand on his khaki trousers. 'Why shouldn't yours be the winning one? Three more numbers and we'll have the draw. A fine china tea set for just one piastre. There's a bargain for you!' 'I'm so lucky, Mummy to have married a real man.' 'A real man? A real bounder, you mean. Work! Work, he says—funny sort of an office that's open till one and two in the morning!' That's what Saber Effendi, their neighbour, had said and Sitt Saniyya, pouring out the coffee, had remarked, 'You see, my poor child, Saber Effendi's had forty years in government service and there's not much that escapes him.'

Lifting Midhat on to his lap, Izzat said softly:

'The child went on having tantrums before he would wash his hands.'

Amal gave him a cold searching look as though seeing him for the first time. She bent her head and concentrated her gaze on a chocolate stain on Midhat's shirt. Izzat appeared to be completely absorbed by teaching the child to count up to ten. Midhat stretched out his hand and put it over his father's mouth. Izzat smiled and leaned towards Amal.

'You know, you look really smart today—pink suits you wonderfully,' he said.

Her throat constricted as she gave a weak smile. Again the old photographer said:

'A picture of you as a group, sir. It'll be very nice and there's no waiting.'

'No thanks,' said Izzat.

Amal spotted the woman in the shorts coming towards them with her swinging gait.

'Let's have a picture taken,' she said in a choked voice.

'What for?'

Aloof, the woman passed her, looking neither at her nor Izzat. She sat down and started talking to her woman friend.

Amal leaned across to Izzat, the words tumbling from her mouth:

'Let's have a picture taken—you and me—let's!' She pointed a finger at him, a finger at herself, and then brought the two fingers together. With a shrug of his shoulder Izzat said:

'Take your picture, old chap.'

When the photogragher had buried his head inside the black hood, Amal stretched her hand and took hold of her husband's arm; as the photographer gave the signal her hand tighened its grip. Waiting for the photograph, Izzat did not look at the woman, nor she at him.

When the photographer came back with the picture, Izzat stood up searching for change.

Amal snatched eagerly at the photograph. She held it in her hand as though afraid that someone would seize it from her. *Izzat at her side—her lover—her husband.* The woman in the shorts pushed back her chair violently as she got to her feet. Passing near to their table, her eyes met those of Amal for a brief instant, fleeting yet suffcient—Amal let the picture fall from her hands. It dropped to the ground, not far from her. Without moving from where she sat propped her elbows on her thighs and her head in her hands, and proceeded to gaze at it with a cool, expressionless face. The picture of the woman looking up at her was that of a stranger, a feverish woman grasping with feverish hand at the arm of a man whose face expressed pain at being gripped so tightly. Slowly, calmly, Amal stretched out her leg and dragged the toe of her shoe, and then the heel, across the photograph. Drawing back her leg and bending down again, she scrutinised the picture anew. Though sand had obliterated the main features, certain portions still remained visible: the man's face grimacing with pain, the woman's hand grasping the man's arm. Amal stretched out her leg and drew the picture close to her chair with her foot till it was within arm's reach. She leaned forward and picked it up.

When Izzat returned with change the picture had been torn into small pieces which had scattered to the winds. The spectrum disappeared and the sun was centrally positioned in the sky, while people were running across the hot sands to avoid burning their feet. Amal realised she had a long way to go.

Caroline's Piece

Letter to my Mother

Dear Mother,

Concentrating deeply on you after all these years gives me a deep sense of sympathy and of love for you. I almost agree with you now about life after death, you always thought of it as a fragmented continuance, parts of the dead annexed by the living. I disagreed with you at the time, but now it seems that of course people don't just stop their involvement in life when they die. You didn't cease to exist when you died, you simply aren't here anymore. So even though you can't reply to this letter, you have some bearing on how it was written, you have some voice in it.

It was through you that I learned who we were, that we were Jews. You had a calm clear way of observing and looking at things, and you told about your childhood carefully with measured words. You never told me I was too young to understand anything, so I was able to listen with a clear mind and fearlessly store away your stories until I would be able to make use of them. By the time I went to school I knew enough not to expect other children to be Jewish, I expected their parents to come from Germany, but already knew that Jews were a minority.

I'd like to tell you a quote from the *Guardian*. It was said at a meeting for concentration camp survivors by a woman who

refusal to grant the truth of a statement

was a prisoner at Auschwitz. She said of the gathering that Not 'There was a denial of the most terrible thing the Germans did to us, namely that many of us identified with the oppressor in the ways that we accepted the picture of the Untermensch* the Nazis were painting of us. Of course we wanted to survive but we weren't at all sure we had the right to survive. We weren't sure that they were wrong about us.'

It is difficult to know on what level such all-pervasive propaganda reaches us. Surely in some way it affected you, together with other forces undermining the will to live. However it always seemed to me that you were sure that the Nazis were evil, that this was something simple and uncomplicated for you.

You often told of the effect the Nazis had on your daily life. How, after a visit from a repairman, who took hours mending your perfectly functioning phone, you always put a tea cosy over the phone because you thought it was bugged. How some SS men stopped you as you were walking down the street with a friend. They sent you home and told your friend not to associate with Jews, it could prove dangerous. You told these details in quiet moments not as lectures with a point, but as episodes that were weighted and had meaning to you.

Your mother complained to the headmaster when a teacher singled you out in class for anti-semitic comments. This alone you thought brave of her. The headmaster promised that the teacher would be told that such anti-semitic behaviour was unacceptable. Apparently he, was because you weren't bothered for a while. Then the headmaster disappeared and anti-semitism reasserted itself. He reappeared six weeks later heavily bandaged, stayed at the school for a week and then finally disappeared and was never seen again. You told this story as an outrage, which it was, but placed the blame where it belonged, with the Nazis and not yourself—it is the sort of thing it would be easy to feel guilty for.

The policeman your family bribed forewarned you when they were coming to collect all male Jews. Your brother and father were sent away separately to hide with friends in the

* *Untermensch*: inferior race

84

country, the lodger was also warned and told not to come home for two days. He returned to fetch something at the same time the Gestapo were re-searching the house, angry at the lack of males. This lodger came back from the concentration camp some months later. He had become insane. Careful nursing by your mother didn't help, he couldn't face reality again, and lived in delusions of grandeur punctuated by utter terror. Although he got out of Germany before it was too late, he lived out the rest of his life in a psychiatric hospital.

I also remember crying when you told how you got one of the last boats out of Germany to Palestine, that the boat after yours was turned away by the British and got bombed in the sea—the refugees died. Now, even remembering the story it seems distant, fact, like so many other atrocities, things that happen to somebody else at another time in another place. But to you it was real and involving and unnecessary, so you made me feel moved by it also.

I grew up with the idea that these things happened, that they were directed at you, that you despised the perpetrators of the atrocities and sympathised deeply with the victims. I got these feelings from you concretely, they were always present in the stories that you told. My problem now is that this knowledge is real to me and sets me apart from the English women I live among. Because I speak fluent accent-free English and was born here, they assume I am one of them, but because of my knowledge of persecution I cannot be.

It strikes me as strange now, that you who were so protective of me in other ways, told me clearly about some of the most terrible dangers of all. I never learnt how those dangers affected you—maybe you didn't either—maybe you thought you could bounce them off your exterior and protect an immutable core. I do know that they affected us all, and that I feel an obligation to you, to the dead Jews, to try and make some sense out of what happened. To try and use my knowledge of the Holocaust positively. I am trying to do this and am deeply grateful to you for telling me truths it might have been easier to hide.

I feel sure that my love can reach you,

Caroline

The Holocaust

What does the Holocaust mean to me?

It is the knowledge that I am only here because my parents managed somehow to escape the fate the world planned for them, because they were part of the minority of European Jews who evaded Gas Chambers. It means before I was even conceived I was a survivor. It is the original guilt in my life compared to which all my other failings and misdeeds shrink almost to nothing.

It is difficult to describe how terrible this knowledge is. There is the fact of it alone, the German super-race gassed the Jewish subhumans and then burnt their bodies while the rest of the world watched. While I might be able to dissociate from the Nazi ideology, and those who carried out these millions of humiliations and murders, how is it possible living in England to dissociate from the people who let my parents' generation of Jews be hounded, tortured and burnt without trying to help.

This awareness of the Holocaust is not something I was told about and then digested and somehow dealt with. It is for me a primordial truth, an intimate knowledge of the existence of pure evil, something I don't think I was ever innocent of and that I will never be able to forget or disregard.

I believe it killed both my parents by drastically lessening their resistance to cancer which they both died of at a relatively young age. It profoundly affected their world views and limited the ways in which they, especially my father, were able to be sensitive to their children.

It has stolen from me the possibility of simple joy and pleasure at being alive. For my existence must always be tainted by the knowledge that my life was bought at incalculable cost in other Jewish lives. I feel an immense pressure to prove myself worthy of an existence bought at such a price.

Ode to the English

Excuse me,
I don't want to embarrass you,
I know it isn't polite to mention these things,
It's just that,
Well,
I'm in pain.
Gas ovens are trying to reclaim me too.
They got my parents in the end
And now they're after me.
No, they won't go away
If I ignore them
We've tried that,
My parents and I
They eat you from inside then,
As cancer or as madness
So what do you suggest?
I know pain isn't English
And you'd prefer me not to mention it,
But you see, it hurts.
It threatens to explode
Then the blood and the ashes
Would go everywhere.
Oh, you do see,
That's why you're standing clear
And averting your eyes
You don't want to be spattered
With the innards of gas ovens
When they burst.

BARBARA BURFORD
Dreaming The Sky Down

She woke bumping gently against the ceiling, like a fair-ground-bought helium filled balloon. Even while she knew it was another waking dream, Donna gloried in the feeling, the light as airiness of her twelve stones drifting way above her bed.

Donna remembered to look especially at her bed this time. No, she was not there. She drifted down closer in the darkness. No, definitely not. She'd have to remember to tell shit-face Dawn Sullivan, that *she* was not having some kind of "primitive spiritualist experience", she *was* dreaming.

She arched her back and did a slow elegant backward roll, skimming the carpet, avoiding the knob on the wardrobe with a skilled half-twist of her swiftly ascending torso.

'Yah!' she whispered triumphantly to her gym teacher, wherever the hell she was. 'Eat your heart out, Miss Howe!' Always going on about how elegant Black athletes were, and how much stamina and natural rhythm they had.

"You must be the exception that proves the rule, Donna!" Hah! Bloody Hah! And everybody else falling about laughing at her.

Yeah, but they should see me now, she thought, as she skimmed the long diagonal of the ceiling, leaving the blue fringes on the lampshade adrift on the wind of her speed. She pushed off from the topmost corner of the room the way the swimmers did it on TV and coasted past her enemy, the mirror, rolling slowly over in order to catch a glimpse of herself as she slipped by.

In the dim glow that was all the curtains let in from the street lamp in the road outside, she saw herself slide by, as elegant as a dolphin. 'A dolphin that wears pyjamas!' she giggled, and drifted back to hang upside down and grin at herself.

I can see my reflection, so at least I'm not a vampire.

She made fangs at herself in the mirror, but had to get up close before she could catch the gleam of her teeth in the glass. She arced over to the light switch, but putting pressure on the toggle ricocheted her backwards towards the ceiling; and only an adroit twist saved her from cannoning off that, flat splat into the wardrobe. She grabbed at her duvet, and when that started to lift, managed to snatch hold of the rail at the bottom of her bed.

She hung there, like a balloon tied to a kid's pushchair, while the racing of her heart steadied. Gradually she remembered how it worked, had always in these dreams, and slowly her feet drifted down till she was no longer upended, but resting lightly at the very top of the pile on the carpet. Very carefully, holding on to the fitted bottom sheet, she got into bed, and pulled the duvet over her. There was still a tendency for her body to bounce gently if she made any sudden movements, so she lay carefully still, eyes wide open, waiting to wake up.

Donna was walking Ben to school before she remembered her dream. She looked down at her younger brother, watching the blue bobble on his knitted hat bounce, as he trotted along beside her. She wondered if Ben dreamed of flying. She couldn't remember dreaming that way until she was nearly thirteen, just after her periods started, in fact. But maybe she had just forgotten, the way she had forgotten the house they lived in when she was younger.

Ben spotted one of his friends, and after checking for traffic, Donna let him tow her across the road, and then charge off along the pavement. But he waited for her at his school gate, and gave her a hug, before he ran to join the playground melée.

Donna liked Ben. The others all complained about their brothers, but despite the fact that she couldn't hang around to chat after school because she had to pick him up, and couldn't have a peaceful laze in the bath without him climbing in *and* bringing his flotilla of empty shampoo bottles, Donna enjoyed having him around.

Gurpreet, Zoe, and Tina were going round to Dawn's house after school to listen to her new *Articulated Donut* LP. Donna pretended nonchalance, insulted their new sex object, the lead singer, by saying he sounded like a frog with one testicle; and set off to collect Ben.

'Frogs don't *have* testicles, Big Bum!' Zoe shouted after her.

'That explains the way he walks then!' Donna got in the last word, before she turned the corner.

At home, she gave Ben his tea, put the TV on for him, and settled down to do her homework before the table was needed for dinner. If she didn't get it done before, she couldn't watch any TV after dinner till it *was* done. And it wasn't any good lying, her mother always checked.

God, what a life! she thought, trying to dredge up what she knew about the Equatorial Forests of Brazil. Everyone else had parents that let them watch TV till all hours, even videos, yet she had to go to bed at nine. According to the others, the discos didn't even start till then. And as for letting her go out with boys, no chance! Not, she reminded herself grumpily, that any had ever expressed an interest in taking her out. And they certainly wouldn't, now that the story of her flooring Zoe's brother at Tina's birthday party was all around the school.

Yeuk! She'd do it again, Donna thought. *"Act like a girl!"* he'd kept saying, pinning he against the wall in the passage squeezing her breasts till they hurt, all the time trying to shove his horrible wet tongue into her mouth.

Her mother came home just before six, and brought her a cup of tea while she was finishing off her English. Donna wished that she looked like her mother, well not exactly like her, she was old after all: Nearly forty! But Donna wished that she too was slim, and could walk without her breasts bouncing. Even in her highest heels, nothing bounced on her mother, when she walked. Yet, she wouldn't let Donna diet, talking about puppy fat.

If I had a puppy this fat, Donna thought sourly, and fourteen years old, I'd shoot it.

Then her dad came in from work and started to chase Ben round the place, so that he could tickle him. Donna, knowing that her dad had only to wriggle his fingers at her, to have her giggling helplessly, removed herself.

Oh, my God! Donna thought, taking refuge in the downstairs toilet. Don't parents ever grow up? And, I wish he'd get another job, so he wouldn't come home on the bus in his railway uniform. It's so *embarrassing* meeting him at the top of the road when he was on early shift.

After she had turned out the light that night, Donna got out of bed and opened the curtains. She did not know if the light streaming in from the sodium street lamp would last into a dream, but it was worth a try. After all, in all her flying dreams, her room was always exactly as it was when she went to sleep.

Donna woke but she knew she was dreaming. She was still under the duvet, and the room was the colour of her mother's amber earrings. Wanting did it, she knew, and gradually she drifted up out of bed, the duvet sliding down her tilting body. She arched her toes, bent backwards from the waist, and turned gently over and over, lifting slowly till her hand brushed the ceiling. She hung suspended turning slowly to look down at her room. It was the same as when she had gone to sleep: her clothes ready for tomorrow over the chair, the book she had been reading in bed, on the bedside table. And the curtains were open!

Donna pushed off from the ceiling, and hung, legs drifting up behind her, one hand clinging to the rim of the sash window. Outside the street was deserted, the leaves on the plane tree across the way rustling secrets at her.

What would it be like, she wondered, to be out there? To drift hand over light hand up the branches of the tree, till she sat in the swaying tufts at the very top? But perhaps it would be scary. Perhaps only the ceiling of her bedroom kept her floating off the world, and out in the open she would begin to fall up off the earth. Even in a dream, that would be scary, Donna decided, and slid away from the window.

For a long time, Donna disported herself in the air of her bedroom, the light from the window gilding her mirrored reflection. She spent ten laughing tumbling minutes trying to get out of her pyjamas in mid-air, before she tethered herself with a foot under her bed rail, and watched her clothes flop to the carpet. They did not float, even in a dream. The phenomenon interested her, and she went down after them, and taking them up to ceiling height, released them. They dropped just as they would have done if she'd tossed them out of the window. She tried several other things. Her pillow was easier to lift than her dictionary; and what's more the book made a sharp noise as it hit the floor.

Donna froze, but there was no response from her parents' room, and soon she was doing lazy naked pinwheels in front of her mirror, trying to see if she could keep the reflected shadow of her navel always in the middle of the glass, while the rest of her moved around her centre.

In the weeks following, despite the occasional snide joking inquiry from the others, Donna no longer wanted to talk about her flying dreams, and the subject was dropped. At home she went to bed promptly, without any of her vast repertoire of procrastinating tactics. Yet, nowadays she seemed extra tired in the mornings, reluctant to get out of bed.

Her mother said it was because she had put on another growing spurt. And indeed she seemed to be growing: upward this time—and despite her increased appetite—not outward; muscles fining out, gaining definition, where once there were just rounded limbs.

Despite this, Miss Howe, once having cast Donna in the role of gymnastic buffoon, still singled her out for ridicule.

'Donna Hamilton!' as Donna clung with a sudden attack of vertigo, unable to tell up from down, to the top of the gym bars. 'You're an absolute disgrace! Have you no pride, girl?'

'Donna Hamilton!' she said today when on dinner duty in

the refectory. 'If you put as much energy into moving the rest of you, as you put into moving your mouth to eat, you wouldn't have all that blubber.'

That night, for the first time, Donna's room could not contain her—her angry energy batting her backwards and forwards between the furniture, the floor, and the ceiling. Finally she gripped the sash of her window to steady her body, through which the storm winds blared, and gazed hungrily out at the space outside.

She tried to turn the knurled knob of the window lock, and turned herself instead. Gradually she added weight to her body, letting her feet sink to the floor, till she could gain purchase on the knob without her body shifting. Quietly, cautiously, she lifted the sash, then lightened until she could swing her body through.

She hung there, at first floor level, one hand clinging to the window frame, then she let go. She bobbed gently, controlling her weight, then with a now skilled flick of her body, she pushed off from the sill in a long shallow dive, lifting as she went. Her reaching hands grasped a handful of summer-dusty plane leaves, and she propelled herself gently, hand over careful hand, along the branch towards the centre of the tree. She added enough weight to let her rest on the branch, and one hand grasping a knobbly outgrowth of the tree trunk, looked down.

Beneath her bare feet, the leaves shifted, green as angelica; restored to springtime translucency by the lamp directly below her. She lightened and drifted carefully up the inner space of the tree, halting once to whisper, in response to startled bird cheeps: 'It's okay! I'm dreaming.'

There was more wind at the top of the tree, and Donna clung to the dipping swaying crown branch, her body curving gently this way and that like a lazy banner. She let go, drifted up, then added weight in a panic, and found herself chin deep in scratchy twigs and leaves, her feet floundering for a hold. Just then, Miss Howe's face, with that sarcastic twist to her lips, flashed across her mind, and Donna let go.

One fisted hand crooked above her head, she exploded up

into the night, her breath escaping in a soundless scream of helpless rage. Then, up where the night wind snapped and pulled at her pyjamas, she slowed, limbs pulling inwards as if on strings, curling in on herself, as she began to tumble slowly, then faster, back towards the skein of orange diamonds that marked the road.

Gradually she regained control, shedding weight, till she stopped with a bob, and began to drift. She was in the open space directly above the road, with nothing to push off from, and her open window away from the direction of the light wind. She lifted, then sent herself in a long sliding slanted glide, her body rolling, turning gently as she added weight to first one side and then the other, beginning to smile, then laugh, the wind of her going cold against her teeth and lips.

With a flick of her wrist, she pulled herself neatly under the sash into her room, remembering to add weight before she slid down the window and thumbed the screw lock fast.

'How on earth did you manage to get those scratches under your chin?' her mother's question at breakfast sent Donna hurtling to the mirror in the kitchen.

'I'm sure they weren't there last night,' her mother came after her. 'You must have done it in your sleep.' She took one of Donna's hands in hers, inspecting her nails. 'You used to do that when you were a baby; scratch yourself. I'll have to make you sleep in mittens again.' But she smiled and gave her a hug.

Donna desperately wanted to go up to her room before she left the house, but her mother was buttoning Ben into his coat, and they always left with her. At the corner, her mother straightened from hugging Ben, and caught Donna gently exploring the scratches with unbelieving fingers.

'Better leave them alone, Donna, or you'll get them infected.' She tilted Donna's chin and looked at the scratches, shaking her head. 'I can't imagine how you got them. We'd better remake your bed tonight, just in case there's a pin or a hairclip in it.'

At school there was assembly, then double maths, before Donna could shut herself in a cubicle in the toilets. She touched the scratches with wondering fingers, then looked carefully at her short cut nails, her smile growing. She closed her eyes, shedding weight gently, lifting until her head was level with the partition. Grinning, she patted herself about the tiny space, promising herself the whole of night sky.

'For chrissake, Donna!' Tina shouted, banging the outer door open. Donna added weight and sunk to the floor so rapidly that she turned her ankle. 'We'll be late, and you know Miss Howe loves you.'

Miss Howe looked as if she had had iron filings for breakfast, and her response to Donna's request that she be excused gym because of her turned ankle, was to turn her around brusquely by the shoulders, and inspect the ankle like a farrier with a horse, before shoving her towards the changing room. All without a word in response.

Donna changed and went in with her commiserating friends. Her heart sank as she saw the range of equipment laid out like an assault course; it was going to be one of *those* sessions.

The first part of the gym session, consisting of gentle stretching exercises, was not too bad, but at the end Donna's ankle was puffing out over her plimsol rim. She watched the others line up and begin their first run at the vaulting horse, with a sinking heart.

She'd hurt herself, she knew she would, she thought, listening to the thumps of their landings.

'Come along, Donna!' Miss Howe was waiting impatiently by the horse.

'I can't!' Donna said. 'My ankle's really hurting now, *and* it's swollen.'

'Nonsense! Come along!'

'No!' Donna took a step backwards, her hands fisting by her sides.

Miss Howe marched over. 'I can't see any swelling or inflammation,' she barely flicked a glance at Donna's ankle. 'You'll use any excuse, won't you?' she sneered.

Donna looked steadily back at her. Just because I'm not pink and white, and bruise like a rainbow; you won't see, will you? But she said nothing.

'Very well. I'm giving you an hour's detention this evening, now go and—'

'But, you can't!' Donna gasped. 'I have to collect my brother from school!'

'You should have thought of that before you were so insolent, shouldn't you? Report to me outside the staffroom at three-thirty.' She turned away.

Donna left school premises during the lunch break, praying that no one would catch her, and tried to get through to Ben's school, but the phone was busy, no matter how many times she dialled. Directory inquiries did not have another number listed for the school, and after several fruitless tries, Donna gave up and snuck dispiritedly back into school. She spent the rest of the day worrying about Ben, and what her parents would say when they found out.

The afternoon lessons dragged, and it was a miracle that she did not collect any more detention orders because of her lack of attention. Her mum would kill her. And Ben... Just the thought of how worried and frightened he would be when she did not turn up to collect him on time made Donna want to burst into tears.

At the end of the afternoon, she waited outside the staffroom, and eventually Miss Howe came along. Donna had considered pleading with her, but one look at that cold antagonistic face stilled the words.

'What is your home room?' Miss Howe contrived to speak at her without looking at her.

'Room Three Twelve, Miss Howe,' Donna filtered any emotion out of her voice.

'Very well. Go to your home room and draw me up a day by day list of everything that you've eaten for the last week. I'll be along presently.' She vanished into the staffroom.

Misery overcoming her rage, Donna climbed slowly back to the third floor, and her empty home room. She had just put her name and the date on the sheet of paper, when a prefect stuck her head round the door.

'Donna Hamilton? Miss Howe says you can go.'

Donna hurtled along the corridor to the staircase at the end, pushing open the swing doors with such force that they swung back and caught her bad ankle. She limped down the first flight of stairs, weak tears welling. Instinctively favouring her bad leg she must have shed weight for she found herself bouncing slightly.

She looked quickly over the banisters; the stairwell was empty. She lifted and slid over the rail and let the weight of her school bag take her purposefully down the well between the flights of stairs. She found she had to hug the bag to her bosom in order not to be dragged head first, and her uniform skirt soon ballooned out, further obstructing her view downwards.

Mary Poppins never has this trouble, she thought aggrievedly, trying to count the flights of stairs as they slid swiftly by.

Miss Howe was standing open-mouthed at the top of the first flight of stairs, hands gripping the banisters, the knuckles gleaming bone white. She made a sudden ineffectual grab at Donna as she slid past, then covered her eyes with both hands, her shoulders cowering up round her ears.

Donna touched down gently, and brushed her skirt down and headed for the outer doors.

'Oh, my God!' Miss Howe's hoarse shout echoed in the stairwell. 'Help! Somebody help! She fell...' Her feet pounded down the stairs and she halted suddenly, horror-struck eyes raking the concrete floor, then lifting, widening, as Donna walked back towards her.

Miss Howe backed, hands going in a warding gesture. 'I came to tell her that her brother's school phoned...and she fell!' And all the time her eyes turned from Donna to the empty concrete floor.

'Who fell, Miss Howe?'

'Donna Hamilton... *You* fell! I saw you!'

'But you couldn't have,' Donna said reasonably, and left to collect Ben.

Ben was waiting forlornly by the locked school gates, when Donna ran breathlessly up. She had shed weight in empty streets, moving in long leaping bounds when there was no one in sight. The schoolkeeper arrived, keys jangling, to let Ben out, and to read Donna a lecture on the "irresponsible kids nowadays". Donna didn't listen, stooping to hug Ben tightly.

When her mother came home that night, Donna immediately told her about being late for Ben.

'Well,' her mother said, fixing her will a stern look. 'It's a good thing you've owned up. One of your teachers phoned me at work, a Miss Howe, she sounded very worried about you. Something about hurting your ankle and getting detention and falling down the stairs,… I couldn't quite understand her. Then the headmistress took over the phone and said that you were going to be a bit late collecting Ben, through your own fault. And that Miss Howe was just upset because she hadn't realised when she gave you detention, quite justifiably that you had to pick up your younger brother.'

Donna felt her heels begin to lift slightly off the floor, and grounded herself so hard that she winced.

'I'll put a compress on your ankle,' her mother guided her into a chair. 'But, first thing tomorrow, you are going to go to the staffroom, and apologise to that teacher.' Her hand lifted Donna's chin, and the stern look was bent on her. 'Do you hear me?'

'Yes, Mum.'

Next morning, Donna waited outside the staffroom while the teachers were arriving. They all ignored her, intent it seemed on gaining the sanctuary of the staffroom. Mrs Pullen, her form mistress came along eventually. 'Donna?' she paused, looking down at one of her better pupils. 'Is there something wrong?'

'I'm waiting for Miss Howe, Mrs Pullen.'

Mrs Pullen looked at the clock above Donnas' head.

'She's usually in by now. Did you knock?'

'No, Mrs Pullen.' Donna shifted her satchel, wishing she was anywhere else in the world.

Mrs Pullen went in, and a minute later Miss Howe came out, carefully closing the door behind her. Donna felt her cold stare like a battering ram, and with an effort met her eyes.

'My mother says I'm to apologise for being rude to you.' she said through stiff lips, and waited to be dismissed.

'Well?'

Donna shouldered her satchel, and at her movement Miss Howe took a step back.

'Well, I'm waiting'

'Can I go now, Miss?'

Miss Howe's face whitened with anger. 'Do you consider that an apology, girl?'

'I apologise, Miss Howe,' Donna said at the point of her shoulder.

'And I do not accept your apology. Now get out of my sight.'

Donna turned abruptly away, feeling eyes like sharp splinters of ice drilling through her back. Her heels lifted slightly, as if to get her out of range as fast as possible. Donna grounded herself, pouring weight on, so that she felt as of she was trying to walk through the polished concrete of the floor.

'Donna!' The voice was cold but insistent. 'What country do you come from?'

Donna turned, meeting those glacial eyes, limpidly, with all the strength of her waking reality.

'Battersea, Miss Howe,' she replied, and walked away.

High in the night sky, with the multicoloured fairy lights of Battersea Bridge directly below her, the cobweb fantasy of Chelsea Bridge beyond that, and the dark squatting bulk of the power station brooding over the oily glisten of the Thames; Donna spoke into the wind:

'Not from outer space, Miss Howe! Not from some strange foreign place, Miss Howe! Battersea, Miss Howe!'

Caving

And there they all were in their dirty blue boiler suits and too big helmets with lights they kept clicking on and off, off and on. There'd been a real scramble for wellies in the boot room. A run on size fives had left a handful of girls to make the best of what was left. They shuffled around insisting they weren't gonna walk nowhere, no way Miss, how would you like it if your boots were three sizes too big. But Miss had brought her own wellies and simply hurried them all up into the bus.

It was an impressive operation for a school outdoor centre. They'd had their talk inside from the young guide who was from South London too.

'I know all about Peckham girls,' he boasted, making them laugh and squirm about in their chairs.

He explained how important it was to keep together in the caves; the biggest danger was joining another school party by mistake because everyone looks the same dressed up in all the gear. He said it wasn't frightening, none of it, if we all keep calm and do what he and Miss say. Their fourteen year old faces looked doubtful.

'The only thing to watch out for,' he warned, his voice growing quiet and serious, 'is the white crocodiles. They're only small mind you, because there isn't any light down there. That's why they're a pale white colour. They can't really hurt you but if your foot drops in the water... well, it takes about fifteen seconds for 'em to feel the vibrations and come to the surface. They nip your ankles a bit.'

'Oh yeah,' said Angie, after a brief scared silence. 'Expect us to believe that?'

'You don't have to believe nothing if you don't want,' he said softly to the silent room. 'Just do as I say when we're underground and we'll be alright. Alright?' He smiled at them, his sharp face opening into a big grin.

'Miss, Miss,' some of them clamoured as they pulled on the clothing. 'It's not true is it? There can't really be crocodiles in the rivers can there?'

Miss said she didn't really know and told them not to worry.

They got to the cave entrance and formed a line.

'Off we go!' he shouted, as they picked their way as delicately as their boots and boiler suits would allow, through a pool of water to the other side of the cave mouth.

'Miss,' he hissed.

She lifted her helmet to hear.

'Always makes me laugh when I see them trying to keep their feet dry. At the end we come back through here and you wait, everyone just sloshes through because by then we're all soaked to the bloody skin.'

He turned back and made them all bunch up together.

'This,' he announced, 'is The Worm Hole. It's hard work, getting to the end, but I know you'll manage. I take little kids and old-people crawling through here no problem.'

So they got on their bellies and knees and elbows and crawled like worms, inch by painful inch. None of them knew rock could be that hard. Little sharp bits sticking up to snag a breast or a hip bone and the only way out is forwards because someone's right behind you. Through the grunting and the swearing one girl's screams took off louder than the rest. Miss was at the back struggling to identify the voice. Could it be Lin? Yes of course. She should have known.

Lin was still screaming when each of them plopped one by one into the first chamber. In the bigger space she began to calm down and stood gulping. Her round red face was streaked with tears and grime, her mouth hung slack and open, dribbling slightly. She held her arms tight across her and sniffed every three seconds or so.

'Oh *god*,' said Tracey impatiently, 'she's always such a baby. Why'd she have to come in *our* group.'

'Don't be so mean,' snapped Angie, roused by a flash of form-group loyalty, 'she's alright, just leave her alone.'

The guide spoke briefly. 'Come on love, it's easier from now on.' And then he ignored her.

Lin went and stood by Miss, right close and waited.

'Which way do we get out of here?' Diane dared to ask. Everyone's voices sounded strange.

'There.' He pointed to a rectangular hole in the wall. It was waist high and small. 'It's called The Letter Box,' he said. 'I'm gonna post you all through it.'

And he did. Head-first they fell into the second chamber screaming and laughing.

'No way,' he said to the first few as they queued up, 'are we gonna get your big bums through here.'

Miss told him that was enough comment on our bodies thank you it's not what we came here for. He shrugged as if to say can't you take a joke, and then good old Julie fed up with waiting shouted, 'Never mind me bum, how am I gonna get my tits through!'

'I've never heard such language from a school party before,' he joked, putting on a posh voice, and they jeered and warned him of worse to come.

'I don't like it down here Miss,' said Lin, as her turn to be posted came closer. But it was either through The Letter Box or crawling back where they'd come from. Miss walked with Lin afterwards, the girl almost twice her size clinging on tight.

'Miss it's like a dark cupboard. I don't like the dark.'

'It's alright Lin,' Miss answered softly. 'I'll get us out of here. Let's just follow the guide for now. Don't worry, we'll be alright.'

They wandered through passages, ducking and bending and then the whole party stopped and crouched on a large platform of rock. The sound of rushing water was everywhere. The guide was like an animal, scuttling about low as if on all fours in his wet-suit skin. He made them huddle round him, before starting with his stories about the early cavers. He told them how back in the 1920s with only candlelight and damp matches they had crawled their way along tortuous cracks and had swum up freezing rivers.

'What *for?*' interrupted someone impatiently.

'For this,' he said, swinging his powerful hand torch around the cavern to light up a whole array of stalactites hanging over a pool of still water. He played his light on the water and told them it takes two hundred years for a stalactite to grow a quarter of an inch.

'And for this,' he said, moving the beam to the limestone walls and ceilings of the chamber. The calcite formations of ancient flowstone seemed to ripple where the light fell. There were streaks of rusty red from iron deposits in the water next to huge green swathes from copper residues that had trickled down for centuries. Zinc and manganese in fierce black lines ran vertically down over the humps and bumps.

'I call them my tapestries,' he said proudly.

'Well I still think they must have been mad to come down here with only a few poxy candles,' Julie muttered to herself.

'Turn your lights off,' said the guide, 'and then you'll get a feel of what it was like when their candles blew out.'

It took a few minutes to get everyone to keep their lights off.

'There,' he said, with satisfaction. 'This is *real* darkness. No matter how long you give your eyes to get used to it, you'll never see no more than you see now.'

Miss remembered another cave, a show cave she went to last year with her lover. The guide there had done the the very same thing only it was on a bigger scale; he threw a switch and all the strings of lights on cable went out. That time in the pitch dark she'd reached for her friend's lips and snatched a full kiss right there under the noses of everyone. One man in the group flicked his zipo lighter and dropped it on the wet ground in his confusion at what he thought he saw. She remembered giggling like the girls and being just so happy standing close to her that day. It seemed nothing could hurt them then. They'd raced to the car afterwards and clambered in laughing and mad for more kissing, not caring at all about the family groups looking and pointing.

'Blimey I'm stiff!' exclaimed Angie as she stretched and banged her head against the rock.

'Keep low,' ordered the guide, leading them on upstream.

Lin still stayed close to Miss, whimpering a little every now and then. Miss held Lin's arm tight wondering what else she should do. Yesterday she'd cradled Angie in her arms at the top of a cliff. The girl was just about to absail down to join her friends at the bottom but sprang back at the last minute, crying and wailing, their helmets and safety harness clunking and crashing together. 'Oh Miss,' she'd cried, 'help me. I don't want to go down.' But Miss had talked her round, slowly and patiently, racked all the while with anxiety about just how far the girls should be pushed to participate in the week's adventurous activities. One morning Sandra and Julie refused to go swimming and then were outraged at not being allowed to canoe in the afternoon. They were doing well though, all of them, and she felt quite proud of her girls, splashing about in these caves, only a few caring that they weren't being seen to their best advantage in boiler suits and hard hats. Julie and Angie especially were right up there next to the guide, being cheeky, trying to make him laugh and notice them. Miss wanted to be up with the guide too. Not stuck at the back again, coaxing and comforting, pushing and pulling. She felt lonely. Even the guide called her Miss. Where's *my* friend to laugh with? she thought, at that moment tired of her responsibilities.

'This is where we stop,' said the guide, 'I said STOP!' They banged into each other, forcing him to take several steps back.

'Here's the ledge that you have to walk along, carefully now, bearing in mind what I told you earlier about the crocodiles. It's not for very far, and they don't bite that hard. Okay!'

He came and took Lin and Miss a different way.

'Miss,' he whispered, pointing to a boulder that looked like an armchair, 'You stay here with Lin. I'm just popping down below for a minute. There's a cave I can reach through from. The water up here's only a few inches deep. I'm gonna be a crocodile.' He slipped off into the darkness.

Meanwhile the girls shuffled along the ledge anxiously, screaming whenever a foot splashed the water they believed to be fathomless.

'It's like bloody James Bond!' Stacey's deep voice bounced off the rocks. 'Like when he has to get past them piranha fish!'

Suddenly their screams changed as the guide grabbed randomly at ankles. Some heaved themselves up onto the rock face, their feet dangling helplessly within reach of the supposed jaw-snapping reptiles. Their tormenter appeared a few seconds later, shouting and frantically shaking his right leg. A small white crocodile had closed its jaws around his ankle.

'It's only plastic!' someone shouted. 'It ain't real!'

'You bastard!' yelled another. 'We nearly died!'

He shrugged off the accusations and told Miss and Lin to stay where they were on the same safe rock. Lin snuggled closer. It was getting cold sitting still.

'He must keep it down here all the time,' said the girl incredulously. 'A little pretend crocodile.' She smiled in the dark, enjoying the escapade now it was over.

'Right,' the guide said to the others when they'd quietened down. 'This is an initiative test. The kind of thing the SAS have to do all the time. It's not easy but I want to see how you get on. Usually the girls do better than the boys on this one.'

'What d'you expect?' said Angie with jeer.

So he put her in front and sent them crawling down another passage with strict instructions to keep their lights off. The test was to crawl in the complete darkness, holding on to the trouser of the one in front, until they felt themselves to be in a big space. They were to wait there in the dark until everyone reached the cave, and then put their lights on. He promised it would be worth it.

'Won't be long Miss,' he said as they set off. 'I'm gonna wait in the cave and give them a bit of a surprise.'

There was a lot of impatient complaining from the tunnel. Shouts of 'How much further is it! Ain't you there yet Angie?' came echoing back to Miss and Lin sitting on their rock.

The scream when it came was unmistakable.

'That's Angie,' Lin whispered to the teacher. 'What's he done to them.'

There was no time to reply. The girls came pouring out of a different hole, indignant and excited.

'Miss, d'you know what he did!' shouted Stacy. 'He was lay-ing there, behind a bleedin' rock, just his legs showing. He was pretending to be a dead body!'

'Yeah an' I was the first to find him,' Angie boasted. 'Any more of them tricks and he will be bloody dead!'

'Not till he's shown us the way out,' Lin said steadily to Miss.

It was alright. The adventure was almost over. After some tired trudging, they were out at the entrance, splashing carelessly through the water as he'd predicted at the start. They all blinked at the sunlight, their dirty faces bursting with stories to tell.

'Look at them, they're all wet!' someone shouted in disgust from the carpark.

The other teacher was waiting with the other half of the group. The guide had to turn around and take the second lot down and play out the same routine all over again. In defiance of strict orders not to tell, some of the first group plucked out their special friends from the second group and handing over helmets and lights quickly told them about the fake crocodile and what else to watch out for.

'Just don't believe nothing he says, I'm telling you,' urged Donna, brave and bold above ground.

'Come on girls,' said Miss, when the second group had dis-appeared from view. 'Let's go for a walk by the river. It's nice and sunny.'

But the girls just wanted to get into the bus and tidy them-selves up and finish off their crisps and sweets from lunch. Miss refused to unlock the bus. No, she told them, not till the others get back. They were immediately furious; some sat down in protest, others moved off and left her with Lin. She could hear them calling her old cow and worse, hating her suddenly. All except Lin. Miss sighed and resigned herself to more of Lin's company. They walked off along the river path in the sunshine, wandering slowly away from the angry scene. As they turned a curve alongside the river's meander, the sun emerged in full force from behind a cloud and soaked them instantly with transforming heat. Miss stopped to pull off some layers of clothing.

'Oh I love it,' she murmured, noticing the full summer foliage by the water's edge; a bright green interspersed with kingcups and meadowsweet. There was even a fluorescent dragon-fly hovering nearby. Everywhere was the scent and colour and texture of childhood holidays; of hours spent at river edges like this one with a net and jar. Marmite sandwiches and warm orange squash. Casting breadcrumbs on the water to lure the minnows close, stretching out and at the last minute the net falls off the bamboo pole and someone gets stung by a wasp and it's never quite how you want it to be. Nothing ever is, she thought, and turned back to look at Lin.

'Oh Miss I'm tired,' said the girl stretching her arms above her head. 'But I like it here. It's nice isn't it? No one else around.'

She took Miss's arm and led her on down the path. Miss was tired too. She let herself be taken, relieved not to have to talk.

'Miss it's the same water isn't it, this water.'

Miss nodded, barely listening.

'It's the same water what goes in the caves, isn't it? Looks different out here.'

'Mmm,' said Miss.

'That guide was quite good really wasn't he, Miss? I mean he was really funny wasn't he? I thought it was good down there.'

Miss looked at the girl, amazed. She wanted to shake her and shout: no he wasn't! He was a bully. You hated him Lin. He terrified you, the caves terrified you. How can you say it was good? How on earth can you forget so quickly?

The girl was still talking, chattering away, oblivious to the effect of her words on Miss.

'I'm gonna send Mr Spencer a card of these caves. I saw them in the shop. He always sends me cards, me and Billy. That's my brother. Mr Spencer sends us birthday cards and Christmas cards.'

'Who's Mr Spencer?' asked Miss, her attention caught now.

'He's the man from the best home me and Billy was ever in. Up in Scotland. You ever been to Scotland Miss?'

'Yes, yes I have.' She stopped herself thinking or saying anything else. She wanted to listen.

'We're back with Mum now,' the girl continued. 'In a flat off

Rye Lane. My mum got married again, to a man from Saudi Arabia but he stays in the bedroom a lot. He likes to do models. Mum calls him a glue sniffer! My mum's quite a laugh you know. She says we all give her grey hairs, which is why she has to dye her hair blonde! She's really pretty you know. Nice and slim, not like me. She says I take after my dad but I've got a nicer nature.'

'You have,' said Miss, her throat catching a little.

Lin was quiet for a minute.

'Miss,' she said earnestly. 'Why are you a teacher?'

'Ahh...' said Miss inarticulately.

'I mean everyone's really horrible to you, aren't they? I'd never be a teacher.'

'No. Well. It's worth it sometimes.' She paused. 'It's really nice when you lot talk to me,' she said smiling, 'and when I've got time to listen.'

Lin turned her head away, pleased and embarrassed.

They walked on in silence for a bit. Miss steered them both round to walk back.

'Tell me about some of the things you like doing,' said Miss conversationally.

'Oh!' burst out the girl enthusiastically. 'I like making plans. I'm gonna come on lots more school journeys Miss, and then when I leave school I'm going back to Scotland. I don't think my mum'll mind. She says sixteen's grown up and I'll have to get on with my own life. I'm going to Scotland to see Mr Spencer. I might have to wait for Billy though. It wouldn't really be fair to go without him...'

Together they walked back along the same path, the sun behind them now. Lin talked and talked, pulling Miss along in tow. One of the other girls appeared in the distance gesturing for them to hurry. Lin moved away from Miss instantly and ran forward waving.

'Hello Cathy!' she shouted excitedly. 'Sorry we're late!'

Eager to be with her friends again, she didn't notice something was funny about the way Cathy came towards them. Miss started to run as soon as she registered the girl's frantic stumbling. She ran and ran, past Lin, past the sobbing Cathy, until the carpark was in sight. Their school bus was completely obscured by the ambulance; flashing and winking it drew her nearer.

'Oh please,' she started to whisper. 'Oh *please* let it be alright.'

ZORA NEALE HURSTON

Their Eyes Were Watching God

Since Tea Cake and Janie had friended with the Bahaman workers in the 'Glades, they, the 'Saws,' had been gradually drawn into the American crowd. They quit hiding out to hold their dances when they found that their American friends didn't laugh at them as they feared. Many of the Americans learned to jump and liked it as much as the 'Saws.' So they began to hold dances night after night in the quarters, usually behind Tea Cake's house. Often now, Tea Cake and Janie stayed up so late at the fire dances that Tea Cake would not let her go with him to the field. He wanted her to get her rest.

So she was home by herself one afternoon when she saw a band of Seminoles passing by. The men walking in front and the laden, stolid women following them like burros. She had seen Indians several times in the 'Glades, in twos and threes, but this was a large party. They were headed towards the Palm Beach road and kept moving steadily. About an hour later another party appeared and went the same way. Then another just before sundown. This time she asked where they were all going and at last one of the men answered her.

'Going to high ground. Saw-grass bloom. Hurricane coming.'

Everybody was talking about it that night. But nobody was worried. The fire dance kept up till nearly dawn. The next day, more Indians moved east, unhurried but steady. Still a blue sky and fair weather. Beans running fine and prices good, so the Indians could be, *must* be, wrong. You couldn't have a hurricane when you're making seven and eight dollars a day picking beans. Indians are dumb anyhow, always were. Another night of Stew Beef making dynamic subtleties with his drum and living, sculptural, grotesques in the dance. Next day, no Indians passed at all. It was hot and sultry and Janie left the field and went home.

Morning came without motion. The winds, to the tiniest, lisping baby breath had left the earth. Even before the sun gave light, dead day was creeping from bush to bush watching man.

Some rabbits scurried through the quarters going east. Some possums slunk by and their route was definite. One or two at a time, then more. By the time the people left the fields the procession was constant. Snakes, rattlesnakes began to cross the quarters. The men killed a few, but they could not be missed from the crawling horde. People stayed indoors until daylight. Several times during the night Janie heard the snort of big animals like deer. Once the muted voice of a panther. Going east and east. That night the palm and banana trees began that long distance talk with rain. Several people took fright and picked up and went in to Palm Beach anyway. A thousand buzzards held a flying meet and then went above the clouds and stayed.

One of the Bahaman boys stopped by Tea Cake's house in a car and hollered. Tea Cake came out throwin' laughter over his shoulder into the house.

'Hello Tea Cake.'

'Hello 'Lias. You leavin', Ah see.'

'Yeah man. You and Janie wanta go? Ah wouldn't give nobody else uh chawnce at uh seat till Ah found out if you all had anyway tuh go.'

'Thank yuh ever so much, Lias. But we 'bout decided tuh stay.'

'De crow gahn up, man.'

'Dat ain't nothin'. You ain't seen de bossman go up, is yuh? Well all right now. Man, de money's too good on the muck. It's liable tuh fair off by tuhmorrer. Ah wouldn't leave if Ah wuz you.'

'Mah uncle come for me. He say hurricane warning out in Palm Beach. Not so bad dere, but man, dis muck is too low and dat big lake is liable tuh bust.'

'Ah naw, man. Some boys in dere now talkin' bout it. Some of 'em been in de 'Glades fuh years. 'Tain't nothin' but uh lil blow. You'll lose de whole day tuhmorrer tryin' tuh git back out heah.'

'De Indians gahn east, man. It's dangerous.'

'Dey don't always know. Indians don't know much uh nothin', tuh tell de truth. Else dey'd own dis country still. De white folks ain't gone nowhere. Dey oughta know if it's dangerous. You better stay heah, man. Big jumpin' dance tuhnight right heah, when it fair off.'

Lias hesitated and started to climb out, but his uncle wouldn't let him. 'Dis time tuhmorrer you gointuh wish you follow crow,' he snorted and drove off. Lias waved back to them gaily.

'If Ah never see you no mo' on earth, Ah'll meet you in Africa.'

Others hurried east like the Indians and rabbits and snakes and coons. But the majority sat around laughing and waiting for the sun to get friendly again.

Several men collected at Tea Cake's house and sat around stuffing courage into each other's ears. Janie baked a big pan of beans and something she called sweet biscuits and they all managed to be happy enough.

Sometime that night the winds came back. Everything in the world had a strong rattle, sharp and short like Stew Beef vibrating the drum head near the edge with his fingers. By morning Gabriel was playing the deep tones in the centre of the drum. So when Janie looked out of her door she saw the drifting mists gathered in the west—that cloud field of the sky—to arm themselves with thunders and march forth against the world. Louder and higher and lower and wider the sound and motion spread, mounting, sinking, darking.

It woke up old Okechobee and the monster began to roll in his bed. Began to roll and complain like a peevish world on a grumble. The folks in the quarters and the people in the big houses further around the shore heard the big lake and wondered. The people felt uncomfortable but safe because there were the seawalls to chain the senseless monster in his bed. The folks let the people do the thinking. If the castles thought themselves secure, the cabins needn't worry. Their decision was already made as always. Chink up your cracks, shiver in your wet beds and wait on the mercy of the Lord. The bossman might have the thing stopped before morning anyway. It is so easy to be hopeful in the day time when you can see the things you wish on. But it was night, it stayed night. Night was striding across nothingness with the whole round world in his hands.

A big burst of thunder and lightning that trampled over the roof of the house. Motor looked up in his angel-looking way and said, 'Big Massa draw him chair upstairs.'

They huddled closer and stared at the door. They just didn't use another part of their bodies, and they didn't look at anything but the door. The time was past for asking the white folks what to look for through that door. Six eyes were questioning *God*.

Through the screaming wind they heard things crashing and things hurtling and dashing with unbelievable velocity. A baby rabbit, terror ridden, squirmed through a hole in the floor and squatted off there in the shadows against the wall, seeming to know that nobody wanted its flesh at such a time. And the lake got madder and madder with only its dikes between them and him.

In a little wind-lull, Tea Cake touched Janie and said, 'Ah reckon you wish now you had of stayed in yo' big house 'way from such as dis, don't yuh?'

'Naw.'

'Naw?'

'Yeah, naw. People don't die till dey time come nohow, don't keer where you at. Ah'm wid mah husband in uh storm, dat's all.'

'Thanky, Ma'am. But 'sposing you wuz tuh die, now. You wouldn't git mad at me for draggin' yuh heah?'

'Naw. We been tuhgether round two years. If you kin see de light at daybreak, you don't keer if you die at dusk. It's so many people never seen de light at all. Ah wuz fumblin' round and

God opened de door.'

He dropped to the floor and put his head in her lap. 'Well then, Janie, you meant whut you didn't say, 'cause Ah never *knowed* you wuz so satisfied wid me lak dat. Ah kinda thought —'

The wind came back with triple fury, and put out the light for the last time. They sat in company with the others in other shanties, their eyes straining against crude walls and their souls asking if He meant to measure their puny might against His. They seemed to be staring at the dark, but their eyes were watching God.

As soon as Tea Cake went out pushing wind in front of him, he saw that the wind and water had given life to lots of things that folks think of as dead and given death to so much that had been living things. Water everywhere. Stray fish swimming in the yard. Three inches more and the water would be in the house. Already in some. He decided to try to find a car to take them out of the 'Glades before worse things happened. He turned back to tell Janie about it so she could be ready to go.

'Git our insurance papers tuhgether, Janie. Ah'll tote mah box mahself and things lak dat.'

'You got all de money out de dresser drawer, already?'

'Naw, git it quick and cut up piece off de tablecloth tuh wrap it up in. Us liable tuh git wet tuh our necks. Cut uh piece uh dat oilcloth quick fuh our papers. We got tuh go, if it ain't too late. De dish can't bear it out no longer.'

He snatched the oilcloth off the table and took out his knife. Janie held it straight while he slashed off a strip.

'But Tea Cake, it's too awful out dere. Maybe it's better tuh stay heah in de wet than it is tuh try tuh —'

He stunned the argument with half a word. 'Fix,' he said and fought his way outside. He had seen more than Janie had.

Janie took a big needle and ran up a longish sack. Found some newspaper and wrapped up the paper money and papers and thrust them in and whipped over the open end with her needle. Before she could get it thoroughly hidden in the pocket of her overalls, Tea Cake burst in again.

"Tain't no cars, Janie.'

'Ah thought not! Whut we gointuh do now?'

'We got tuh walk.'

'In all dis weather, Tea Cake? Ah don't b'lieve Ah could make it out de quarters.'

'Oh yeah you kin. Me and you and Motor Boat kin all lock arms and hold one 'nother down. Eh, Motor?'

'He's sleep on de bed in yonder,' Janie said. Tea Cake called without moving.

'Motor Boat! You better git up from dere! Hell done broke loose in Georgy. Dis minute! How kin you sleep at uh time lak dis? Water knee deep in de yard.'

They stepped out in water almost to their buttocks and managed to turn east. Tea Cake had to throw his box away, and Janie saw how it hurt him. Dodging flying missiles, floating dangers, avoiding stepping in holes and warmed on the wind now at their backs until they gained comparatively dry land. They had to fight to keep from being pushed the wrong way and to hold together. They saw other people like themselves struggling along. A house down, here and there, frightened cattle. But above all the drive of the wind and the water. And the lake. Under its multiplied roar could be heard a mighty sound of grinding rock and timber and a wail. They looked back. Saw people trying to run in raging waters and screaming when they found they couldn't. A huge barrier of the makings of the dike to which the cabins had been added was rolling and tumbling forward. Ten feet higher and as far as they could see the muttering wall advanced before the braced-up waters like a road crusher on a cosmic scale. The monstropolous beast had left his bed. The two hundred miles an hour wind had loosed his chains. He seized hold of his dikes and ran forward until he met the quarters; uprooted them like grass and rushed on after his supposed-to-be conquerors, rolling the dikes, rolling the houses, rolling the people in the houses along with other timbers. The sea was walking the earth with a heavy heel.

'De lake is comin'!' Tea Cake gasped.

'De lake!' In amazed horror from Motor Boat, 'De lake!'

'It's comin' behind us!' Janie shuddered. 'Us can't fly.'

'But we still kin run,' Tea Cake shouted and they ran. The gushing water ran faster. The great body was held back, but rivers spouted through fissures in the rolling wall and broke like day. The three fugitives ran past another line of shanties that topped a slight rise and gained a little. They cried out as best they could, 'De lake is comin'!' and barred doors flew open and others joined them in flight crying the same as they went. 'De lake is comin'!' and the pursuing waters growled and shouted ahead, 'Yes, Ah'm comin'!' and those who could fled on.

They made it to a tall house on a hump of ground and Janie said, 'Less stop heah. Ah can't make it no further. Ah'm done give out.'

'All of us is done give out,' Tea Cake corrected. 'We'se goin' inside out dis weather, kill or cure.' He knocked with the handle of his knife, while they leaned their faces and shoulders against the wall. He knocked once more then he and Motor-Boat went round to the back and forced a door. Nobody there.

'Dese people had mo' sense than Ah did,' Tea Cake said as they dropped to the floor and lay there panting. 'Us oughta went on wid 'Lias lak he ast me.'

'You didn't know,' Janie contended. 'And when yuh don't know, yuh just don't know. De storms might not of come sho nuff.'

They went to sleep promptly but Janie woke up first. She heard the sound of rushing water and sat up.

'Tea Cake! Motor Boat! De lake is comin'!'

The lake *was* coming on. Slower and wider, but coming. It had trampled on most of its supporting wall and lowered its front by spreading. But it came muttering and grumbling onward like a tired mammoth just the same.

'Dis is uh high tall house. Maybe it won't reach heah at all,' Janie counselled. 'And if it do, maybe it won't reach tuh de upstairs part.'

'Janie, Lake Okechobee is forty miles wide and sixty miles long. Dat's uh whole heap uh water. If dis wind is shovin' dat whole lake disa way, dis house ain't nothin' tuh swaller. Us better go. Motor Boat!'

'Whut you want, man?'

'De lake is comin'!'

'Aw, naw it 'tain't.'

'Yes, it is *so* comin'! Listen! You kin hear it way off.'

'It kin jus' come on. Ah'll wait right here.'

'Aw, get up, Motor Boat! Less make it tuh de Palm Beach road. Dat's on uh fill. We'se pretty safe dere.'

'Ah'm safe here, man. Go ahead if yuh wants to. Ah'm sleepy.'

'Whut you gointuh do if de lake reach heah?'

'Go upstairs.'

'S'posing it come up dere?'

'Swim, man. Dat's all.'

'Well, uh, Good bye, Motor Boat. Everything is pretty bad, yuh know. Us might git missed of one 'nother. You sho is a grand friend fuh uh man tuh have.'

'Good bye, Tea Cake. Y'all oughta stay here and sleep, man. No use in goin' off and leavin' me lak dis.'

'We don't wanta. Come on wid us. It might be night time when de water hem you up in heah. Dat's how come Ah won't stay. Come on, man.'

'Tea Cake Ah got tuh have mah sleep. Definitely.'

'Good bye, then, Motor. Ah wish you all de luck. Goin' over tuh Nassau fuh dat visit widja when all dis is over.'

'Definitely, Tea Cake. Mah mama's house is yours.'

Tea Cake and Janie were some distance from the house before they struck serious water. Then they had to swim a distance, and Janie could not hold up more than a few strokes at a time, so Tea Cake bore her up till finally they hit a ridge that led on towards the fill. It seemed to him the wind was weakening a little so he kept looking for a place to rest and catch his breath. His wind was gone. Janie was tired and limping, but she had not had to do that hard swimming in the turbulent waters, so Tea Cake was much worse off. But they couldn't stop. Gaining the fill was something but it was no guarantee. The lake was coming. They had to reach the six-mile bridge. It was high and safe perhaps.

Everybody was walking the fill. Hurrying, dragging, falling, crying, calling out names hopefully and hopelessly. Wind and rain beating on old folks and beating on babies. Tea Cake stumbled once or twice in his weariness and Janie held him

117

up. So they reached the bridge at Six Mile Bend and thought to rest.

But it was crowded. White people had pre-empted that point of elevation and there was no more room. They could climb up one of its high sides and down the other, that was all. Miles further on, still no rest.

They passed a dead man in a sitting position on a hummock, entirely surrounded by wild animals and snakes. Common danger made common friends. Nothing sought a conquest over the other.

Another man clung to a cypress tree on a tiny island. A tin roof of a building hung from the branches by electric wires and the wind swung it back and forth like a mighty ax. The man dared not move a step to his right lest this crushing blade split him open. He dared not step left for a large rattlesnake was stretched full length with his head in the wind. There was a strip of water between the island and the fill, and the man clung to the tree and cried for help.

'De snake won't bite yuh,' Tea Cake yelled to him. 'He skeered tuh go intuh uh coil. Skeered he'll be blowed away. Step round dat side and swim off!'

Soon after that Tea Cake felt he couldn't walk anymore. Not right away. So he stretched long side of the road to rest. Janie spread herself between him and the wind and he closed his eyes and let the tiredness seep out of his limbs. On each side of the fill was a great expanse of water like lakes—water full of things living and dead. Things that didn't belong in water. As far as the eye could reach, water and wind playing upon it in a fury. A large piece of tar-paper roofing sailed through the air and scudded along the fill until it hung against a tree. Janie saw it with joy. That was the very thing to cover Tea Cake with. She could lean against it and hold it down. The wind wasn't quite so bad as it was anyway. The very thing. Poor Tea Cake!

She crept on hands and knees to the piece of roofing and caught hold of it by either side. Immediately the wind lifted both of them and she saw herself sailing off the fill to the right, out and out over the lashing water. She screamed terribly and released the roofing which sailed away as she plunged downward into the water.

'Tea Cake!' He heard her and sprang up. Janie was trying to swim but fighting water too hard. He saw a cow swimming slowly towards the fill in an oblique line. A massive built dog was sitting on her shoulders and shivering and growling. The cow was approaching Janie. A few strokes would bring her there.

'Make it tuh de cow and grab hold of her tail! Don't use yo' feet. Jus' yo' hands is enough. Dat's right, come on!'

Janie achieved the tail of the cow and lifted her head up along the cow's rump, as far as she could above water. The cow sunk a little with the added load and thrashed a moment in terror. Thought she was being pulled down by a gator. Then she continued on. The dog stood up and growled like a lion, stiff-standing hackles, stiff muscles, teeth uncovered as he lashed up his fury for the charge. Tea Cake split the water like an otter, opening his knife as he dived. The dog raced down the back-bone of the cow to the attack and Janie screamed and slipped far back on the tail of the cow, just out of reach of the dog's angry jaws. He wanted to plunge in after her but dreaded the water, somehow. Tea Cake rose out of the water at the cow's rump and seized the dog by the neck. But he was a powerful dog and Tea Cake was over-tired. So he didn't kill the dog with one stroke as he had intended. But the dog couldn't free himself either. They fought and somehow he managed to bite Tea Cake high up on his cheek-bone once. Then Tea Cake finished him and sent him to the bottom to stay there. The cow relieved of a great weight was landing on the fill with Janie before Tea Cake stroked in and crawled weakly upon the fill again.

Janie began to fuss around his face where the dog had bitten him but he said it didn't amount to anything. 'He'd uh raised hell though if he had uh grabbed me uh inch higher and bit me in mah eye. Yuh can't buy eyes in de store, yuh know.' He flopped to the edge of the fill as if the storm wasn't going on at all. 'Lemme rest awhile, then us got tuh make it on intuh town somehow.'

ALICIA PARTNOY

The Little School

The One-Flower Slippers

That day, at noon, she was wearing her husband's slippers; it was hot and she had not felt like turning the closet upside down to find her own. There were enough chores to be done in the house. When they knocked at the door, she walked down the ninety-foot corridor, *flip-flop, flip-flop*. For a second she thought that perhaps she should not open the door; they were knocking with unusual violence...but it was noon time. She had always waited for them to come at night. It felt nice to be wearing a loose house dress and his slippers after having slept so many nights with her shoes on, waiting for them.

She realised who was at the door and ran towards the back-yard. She lost the first slipper in the corridor, before reaching the place where Ruth, her little girl, was standing. She lost the second slipper while leaping over the brick wall. By then the shouts and kicks at the door were brutal. Ruth burst into tears in the doorway. While squatting in the bushes, she heard the shot. She looked up and saw soldiers on every roof. She ran to the street through weeds as tall as she. Suddenly the sun stripped away her clothing; it caught her breath. When the soldiers grabbed her, forcing her into the truck, she glanced down at her feet in the dry street dust; afterward she looked up: the sky was so blue that it hurt. The neighbours heard her screams.

The floor of the truck was cool, but the tiles at Army Head-quarters were still cooler. She walked that room a thousand times from one end to the other until they came to take her. Through a peep hole under her blindfold she could see her feet on the tiny black and white tiles, the stairs, the corridor. Then came the trip to the Little School.

At the concentration camp kitchen they listed her belongings. 'What for, if you are going to steal them all?' she asked.

'A wedding ring, a watch...dress colour...bra...she doesn't wear one...shoes...she doesn't have any.'

'She doesn't? It doesn't matter, she won't have to walk much.' Loud guffaws.

She was not paying attention to what they were saying. She did try to guess how many of them there were. When she thought the interrogation session was about to begin, they took her to a room. She walked down a tiled corridor, then an old wooden floor. After arriving at the wretched bed assigned to her, she discovered a ragged blanket. She used it to cover her feet and did not feel so helpless.

The following morning someone tapped her on the shoulder and made her stand up. Someone had re-tied her blindfold during the night. The peep hole was smaller but still big enough for her to see the floor: blood on the tiles next to a spot of sky blue. They made her walk on the blood; she tried not to avoid it so they would not notice that she could see.

While they opened the iron grate into the corridor, she thought for a minute of the sky blue spot. She could have sworn that it was a very familiar colour, like the sky blue colour of her husband's pants. It was the same sky blue of his pants; it *was* him, lying on the hall floor, wounded. Her heart shrank a little more until it was hard as a stone. 'We must be tough,' she thought, 'otherwise they will rip us to shreds.' Fear carved an enormous hole in her stomach when she stepped down onto the cement floor of the "machine" room and saw the side of the metal framed bed like those used for torture.

She does not remember exactly the day it all happened. In any event, she already knew by then something about the pace of life at the Little School. She knew, for example, that after mealtimes, if they were allowed to sit for a short while on the edge of the bed, she could, without being caught, whisper a few words out of the side of her mouth to Vasquita, who was in the bunk next to hers. She chose the words.

'Vasca,' she called out.

'Yes...'

'They gave me some slippers with only one flower.'

'At last.'

'Did you understand me? Just one flower, two slippers and just one flower.'

Vasca stretched her neck and lifted up her face to peek under her blindfold. The flower, a huge plastic daisy, looked up at them from the floor. The other slipper, without a flower, was more like them. But the one-flowered slipper amid the dirt and fear, the screams and the torture, that flower so plastic, so unbelievable, so ridiculous was like a stage prop, almost obscene, absurd, a joke.

Vasca smiled first, then laughed, it was a nervous and barely restrained laughter. If she were caught laughing, it was going to be very hard to explain what was so funny. Then blows would come, with or without explanations.

She shuffled the daisy around for more than a hundred days, from the latrine to the bed, from the bed to the shower. Many times she blindly searched under the bed for the daisy in between the guards' shouts and blows.

The day she was transferred to prison, someone realised that she should be wearing "more decent" shoes. They found her a pair of tennis shoes three sizes too big. The one-flowered slippers remained at the Little School, disappeared...

Graciela: Around the Table

Fifteen days ago this business of walking around the table began. At least it's something different to do every afternoon. I've already walked around the table eight times today. Two more steps to the edge...I feel a little dizzy...Now in the opposite direction: *one, two, three, four, five, six...one, two, three, four...one, two...*

'What name did you choose, ma'am?'

What a question! As if they cared. I must admit that now they feel some sort of compassion; they no longer beat or molest me. In fact, I've just realised that for the past few days they haven't screamed at me either. Well, with this huge belly! But they weren't worried about my belly when they arrested me. The trip from Cutral-Co to Neuquén was pure hell... They knew I was pregnant. It hadn't occurred to me that they could torture me while we were travelling. They did it during the whole trip: the electric prod on my abdomen because they knew about the pregnancy... *One, two, three, four...* Each shock brought that terrible fear of miscarriage...and that pain, my pain, my baby's pain. I think it hurt more because I knew he was being hurt, because they were trying to kill him...Sometimes I think it would have been better if I had lost him.

Twelve rounds already. I wonder whether this "exercise program" is just one more sham or if they'll let me live until my child is born. And what after that? Better not to think for a while... The thirteenth time around the table. The "doctor" prescribed thirty. He may not even be a doctor. How could a doctor be an accomplice? That was a stupid thought. There can be assassins in any field.

The twentieth time around this table. Somebody is asking for water. It's María Elena's voice. María Elena, so little and so strong, so determined to fight injustice: 'We must do something sister,' she said. I guess she was repeating what she'd heard from Raul and me. I thought I was going to loose my mind when they brought her to the Little School. When I noticed that they suspected she was involved, I imagined a thousand ways of warning her, all of them impossible, there was no escape... That's why when they brought in Alicia, the first thing I thought was to ask her if she still had any communication with the outside world. In Hell there probably isn't any communication with the outside world either. Now the guilt feelings... one more chain, the blindfold around my eyes, the gauze around my hands... At times I would like to disappear—to truly disappear—to fly away with the wind that blows through the window, to vanish from the world.

The baby walks around this table with me, within me... Four more rounds to go. I'm already exhausted from walking, no breath left... I know this table by heart, I'd pick it out from all the tables of the world, even if I could never see it well. Thirty rounds, fifteen days... four hundred and fifty rounds... Today my blindfold is very tight and I can't even see my feet or the dress with the flowered pattern. Who was the owner of this dress? The child is moving... my love, to protect you, my dear child? Me?... so unprotected myself. If only your father were here. Perhaps you could hear his whispers, 'Be strong my child, take heart... The future is yours.' Your future, my child... we gave up sunshine on our skin for your future... The thirtieth round of this living death. Don't forgive them, my child. Don't forgive this table either.

A Conversation Under the Rain

This day had been different: the rain had made it different. Shortly after lunch it had begun to rain. The smell of damp earth made her come to grips with the fact that she was still alive. She inhaled deeply and a rare memory of freedom tickled her cheekbones. The open window let some rain in... A drop fell on her forehead, just above the blindfold, and slowly began to make its way to her heart. Her heart, hard as stone, after having shrunk to dodge anguish, finally softened. Like day-old bread soaking in water, her heart was swelling and dissolving, slowly but unavoidably... When she thought she was about to cry, she heard her window close.

The Little School was full of roof leaks; she had confirmed this while she was still in the other room, when it rained cats and dogs in January. On that day, water had fallen in buckets on the bunk beds; it had been cold. This time, on the contrary, rain was just beginning to fall. When almost as many drops had fallen as the days she had spent there, they placed cans under the leaks. The first four cans were making the sweetest music she had heard in a very long time. For a while she concentrated on figuring our the frequency of the drops: *clink*...

clonk ... plunkplunk ... clink ...clonkpluck ... plunk ... clink ...clonk ...plop...plop... Can number one was near the back window, the one that had been boarded up. The second can was by Vasca's bed, the third was right in the centre of the room, and the fourth was probably by the door frame. Suddenly she heard; *drip... drip... drip...* She stretched out her hand and the drops found a place in her palm. She treasured five of them in the hollow of her hand, five little pools of freshness and life among all that dirtiness... She washed her hands. That contact with water, the first in more than twenty days, made her feel as if she was also washing away some of the bitterness that—mixed with filth—was clinging to her skin. She used the next few drops to wet her lips.

'María Elena,' she called out.

'Yes...' the answer came back in a whisper.

'I own a leak.'

'Me, too.'

The leaks had multiplied after supper.

First, they moved María Elena's bed towards hers; after a while—leaks pelted her bed on all sides—they also had to move her bed. When the guard left, she called María Elena again. Happiness filled her body when she heard María Elena's voice only four feet from her head.

'We're very close.'

For the first time in more than two months the guards had placed her next to someone else's bed. Both women's heads were facing in the same direction. The guard had forgotten to make them lie with their heads in opposite directions... perhaps it had been an intentional omission.

'Where is he?'

'I don't hear him.'

'I heard him leave.'

'Could we talk?'

'I guess so, we're really close, he can't hear us.'

'The sound of water helps to conceal our voices...'

'It feels like we're paying each other a social visit.'

They silently laughed, feeling comfortable in their bunk beds, and ready to enjoy some chatting. They sighed at the same time, relaxing. They laughed again. She had not been able to talk to María Elena for two days; the last time, in a rush, she had given María Elena some ideas about yoga.

'Could you sleep?'

'Yes! It was fantastic. I breathed rhythmically as you'd told me, then I was so busy noticing the muscles of my body, relaxing them and feeling them heavily sink in to the mattress that for a while I even forgot where I was.'

'What about the other problem?'

'I haven't menstruated yet. I'm worried. I think I'm pregnant.'

'Don't worry, wait some more. Remember that none of us are menstruating. Vasca, for example, hasn't for five months ... but she isn't pregnant. I don't menstruate either, and also María Angélica... I don't know, it's as if our bodies were protecting themselves...'

'I told the "doctor" yesterday. He said that he'll give us all injections so we become regular, but that he'll do it the day we're sent to prison.'

Silence.

'Did you hear me?'

Silence. 'María Elena?' she heard María Elena clear her throat and look for her shoes under the bed. Then she knew it. She held her breath and froze, waiting. She felt a hand like a hook on her shoulder. 'Get up! Put your slippers on.'

Peine took her to the kitchen. He didn't say a word. It might have been eleven at night, and it was silent at the Little School. They walked through the iron grate and the wooden door. When they got there, Peine ordered the other guard:

'Untie her hands.'

She summoned all her defenses, blocking out any speculation about her fate. She did not indulge in self-pity. The hatred she felt for them shielded her. She waited.

'Take off your clothes.'

She stood in her underwear, her head up. She waited.

'All clothes off, I told you.'

She took off the rest of her clothes. She felt as if the guards did not exist, as if they were just repulsive worms that she could erase from her mind by thinking of pleasant things... like rain falling inside the cans, her conversation with María

Elena. She thought the conversation had been worth it, despite the beatings that could come, despite humiliation. They tied her hands behind her back.

One by one, the drops on her skull were telling her a ridiculous story, a story that made her laugh just because she was not allowed to laugh. Those two killers had been glancing through the pages of an encyclopedia. On the Chinese history page, they had seen a drawing of the Chinese torture method "the drop of water", puzzled to see that there still existed tortures that they had not used, they wanted to try this one to see how it worked.

Chinese torture under a roof leak!... Black humour made her shield thicker and more protective. Drops of water sliding down her hair dampened the blindfold on her eyes. Threats and insults sliding down her shield shattered into pieces on the kitchen floor.

She thought of little María Elena. When they first met, María Elena was only fifteen. Five years older and carrying a baby in her womb, she had become motherly with the teenagers in her theatre classes. Two years later she was still feeling the need to protect María Elena, the girl who had dreamt of knitting socks for the baby and found sweet names for it. She did not know that María Elena was involved in politics. However, she had some hints: her way of debating in class discussions, the kind of controversies that María Elena helped to stimulate. Her intuition proved correct the time they had run into each other in the street. It had been a coincidence; both of them had excuses, obviously, to take off in a hurry for their meetings.

Underneath the roof leak she was thinking of María Elena, her brand new seventeen years, her flight towards a future caught in that cage of death. Half an hour later they untied her hands.

'Put your clothes on.'

She dressed very fast, as if she had suddenly become aware of her nakedness. In the corridor that led to the iron grate, Peine kicked her roughly several times. She thought he was mad because she had neither cried nor pleaded for mercy, because she had not even trembled. She thought he was upset because in spite of the blows and restraints, in spite of the filth and torture, both women had had that long and warm conversation under the rain.

Religion

Yesterday, when Abuelo caught me talking, he took me to Chiche. Chiche was sitting in the hall, pounding his horse whip on the edge of the table. He made me stand two feet from him. I could see his legs from underneath my blindfold.

'I heard you're a Jew, is that right?'

'Yes, sir.'

'Okay. If you don't behave we're going to make soap out of you, understand?'

I was expecting him to whip me, but he didn't. Abuelo brought me back to my bunk bed.

Chiche's warning didn't frighten me, maybe because I'm convinced that at the Little School there isn't sufficient technology to make soap out of anybody. Perhaps I didn't take him seriously because I already knew I could be killed at any moment.

Now that Chiche has come out with the "discovery" of my Jewishness, I realise this is the first time the subject of my race has come up here. When I was interrogated the guards didn't mention it at all. In any case it's not for being Jewish that I was brought to the Little School. Néstor and Mary weren't brought here because they are Christian either. So many priests have blessed the weapons of the military! So many rabbis thank God for the coup that has saved them from "chaos!" Whenever things like this happen, I'm convinced that God is just a pretext...and I instinctively reject pretexts.

Since yesterday, when Abuelo caught me talking and took me before Chiche, I haven't even tried to open my mouth. A short while ago the guards were changed; Peine is in the hall now. He hasn't found me talking yet. I can still take a chance.

'Vasca,' I whisper...

Nativity

'Sir, when's the doctor coming?'
The labour pains and contractions are almost constant, very close together. This child wants to get out. What will they do to me after it's born? They've said they'll transfer me to a regular prison where I'll be able to take care of the baby. I'm scared...

'Don't worry, ma'am, everything is going to be alright.'
'Don't I have reason to worry, being in your hands?'

Today I was sitting in the backyard; it was a sunny day. My eyes without blindfold, looking at the garage door. Out there, just sixty feet away, freedom. How does it feel to be free? I can't even remember. And the doctor isn't coming... The sunshine, the trees, everything seemed to be so good in the backyard this morning... For a second I thought I was on the other side of the door... The contractions are coming more frequently... The child is going to be born.

'Where's the doctor?'
'He'll probably be late, but don't worry, I know enough about these matters.'
Jesús! He's pushing... Don't take him away... If only I could keep my baby inside... Ugh... Now I have to push, if I don't it hurts more. If we could survive, my child... If we survive...

A new cry makes its way through the shadows fighting above the trailer. Graciela has just given birth. A prisoner child has been born. While the killers' hands welcome him into the world, the shadow of life leaves the scene, half a winner, half a loser: on her shoulders she wears a poncho of injustice. Who knows how many children are born every day at the Little School?

Peter

WINNIE MANDELA

*D*etention and Trial, 1969

In May 1969 Winnie Mandela and twenty-one men and women were detained in nationwide dawn raids under the Terrorism Act.* She was to spend 491 days in detention, most of it in solitary confinement. They were then charged under the Suppression of Communism Act with 'furthering the aims of an unlawful organisation' and the state alleged that 'the accused acted in concert and with a common purpose to re-establish and build up the National African Congress (ANC), knowing that its ultimate aim was the violent overthrow of the state'. The ninety-nine counts ranged from giving the ANC salute, singing ANC songs, recruiting members, discussing or possessing ANC literature, to 'polluting' the youth.

The evidence of state witnesses was unconvincing; it became obvious that they had been tortured and forced to make incriminating state-ments. The state withdrew all the charges, and on 16 February 1970 Win-nie Mandela and the other defendants were all acquitted.

As they prepared to leave the court, they were re-detained, under Section 6 of the Terrorism Act. Not until June, and only after widespread protests, were Mrs Mandela and nineteen others finally charged under that Act. Almost all the charges were repetitions of those on which they had already been acquitted. Again, on 14 September 1970, they were all acquitted.

Within two weeks Winnie Mandela was served with a new, five-year banning order restricting her to Orlando West and placing her under house arrest each night and during weekends and public holidays. She

---

* The Terrorism Act, No. 83 of 1967, empowers the South African police to arrest any person suspected of committing acts endangering the maintenance of law and order or conspiring or inciting people to commit such acts. The Act is so loosely defined that almost any opponent of the South African regime can be arrested without a warrant, detained for interrogation and kept in solitary confinement without access to a lawyer or relative for an indefinite period of time. Children are not exempted.

130

was served with the new bans just as she was leaving for Robben Island to visit her husband, whom she had not seen for two years.

In the years that followed there were frequent attacks on her life and property: on one occasion a gunman was found in her yard, on another her house was broken into; a petrol bomb was hurled through a window; her watchdog was poisoned; and one night three men broke in and attempted to strangle her. Her daughter Zindzi appealed to the United Nations to call on the South African Government to protect her mother.

I was detained on 12 May 1969. Detention means that midnight knock when all about you is quiet. It means those blinding torches shone simultaneously through every window of your house before the door is kicked open. It means the exclusive right the Security Branch have to read each and every letter in the house. It means paging through each and every book on your shelves, lifting carpets, looking under beds, lifting sleeping children from mattresses and looking under the sheets. It means tasting your sugar, your mealie-meal and every spice on your kitchen shelf. Unpacking all your clothing and going through each pocket. Ultimately it means your seizure at dawn, dragged away from little children screaming and clinging to your skirt, imploring the white man dragging Mummy away to leave her alone.

We were the first prisoners under Section 6 of the Terrorism Act. I was kept in Pretoria Central Prison. My cell had a grille inside, a door in the middle and another grille outside. From what I heard and had read I realised that mine must be the death cell. I did not even know I was with other detainees in the same block. I thought I was alone; for months I didn't know that the whole country had been rounded up. All I could hear was a distant cough and a faint sound of prison doors being locked.

Those first few days are the worst in anyone's life—that uncertainty, that insecurity: there is such a sense of hopelessness, the feeling that this is now the end. The whole thing is calculated to destroy you, not only morally but also physically. You knew the enemy could keep you there for five years. You are not in touch with anybody. And in those days all I had in the cell was a sanitary bucket, a plastic bottle which could contain only about three glasses of water, and a mug.

Sometimes they would bring a little plastic bucket with water to wash yourself, but you didn't get any water to wash your clothes. They must have been sanitary buckets because the smell was terrible. They weren't even properly rinsed. So I used the drinking water from the plastic bottle to wash my face. And I had to use my panties to wash my body because there was nothing else. During menstruation we only got toilet paper or they would say, 'Go and use your big fat hands.' For a bed there was only a mat and three stinking filthy blankets. I rolled one up for a pillow and slept with the other two.

The days and nights became so long I found I was talking to myself. It is deathly quiet—that alone is a torture. You don't know what to do with yourself; you sit down, you stand up, you pace up and down. The cell is so small that you can't even run right round. You lie on your stomach, you lie on your back, on your side; your body becomes sore, because you are not used to sleeping on cement. What kept me going in the cells were the Canadian Air Force exercises for women—I'm addicted to those, I couldn't live without them.

You find yourself looking for anything in the cells; for instance, I remember how happy I was when I found two ants, how I spent the whole day with these ants, playing with them on my finger and how sad I was when the warders switched off the light. That was during the day, but the building was so old that it was perpetually dark. Then there was nothing else to do. So I started ripping one of those blankets, pulling out the threads and making little ropes. I spent whole days making them and undoing them. Then I undid the hem of my dress, just to have something to do. After that there was nothing else to do.

At night it was not possible to sleep. They kept the light on, but also I had been suffering from acute insomnia for some years. During interrogation through the night Swanepoel* referred to that and said, 'We are providing company for you all night long and you are ungrateful.'

We had inspection every day in prison. Two wardresses

* One of the most notorious members of the Security Police; a number of detainees interrogated by him alleged torture.

walk in, they order you to stand up, they take off your clothes. They start by inspecting your shoes as you stand there stark naked. They go through your panties, your bra, they go through every seam of every garment. Then they go through your hair and – of course, they never succeeded with me, but with female prisoners it's common practice – they inspect the vagina. I don't think they did that to my other five comrades who were also in that prison. Nothing is more humiliating. And you are all alone in that cell.

When I got permission to get a few clothes from relatives, the process now took twice the amount of time.

I was so angry. I considered just about everything I could do to myself as a form of protest. If I didn't have children, and if it wasn't for the fact that I would be playing into the authorities' hands, I might have taken my life. But one would be doing this for people who have no conscience at all.

My interrogation started on a Monday. And I was only delivered back to the cell on the Saturday night. They interrogated me for five days and five nights. I remember that vaguely. During the fifth night I was having these fainting spells which are very relieving. It was the first time I realised that nature has a fantastic way of providing for excess exhaustion of the body. I just had these long blackouts; I must have been delivered back in the cell during one of them. We were interrogated continuously. My whole body was badly swollen, I was passing blood. There were times when one was allowed to go to the toilet, but very briefly, and a woman wardress would actually go into the toilet with you.

They do give you something to eat, but you can't eat under those circumstances—food is of no relevance. The whole experience is so terrible, because I had left little children at home in bed and I had no idea what had happened to them.

The interrogation was about the activities of the banned African National Congress, and the 'communist' contacts we were supposed to have outside. Of course, a lot of activities had been taking place, activities which in a democratic country are everyone's rights. We had informal education groups and meetings, which take place in every country.

Swanepoel said some of the most extraordinary things to

me during interrogation: 'You are going to be broken completely, you are shattered, you are a finished woman.' And: 'You know, people think Nelson is a great man, they think he is in prison because he wanted to sacrifice for his people. If I had a wife like you, I would do exactly what Nelson has done and go and seek protection in prison. He ran away from you. What kind of woman holds meetings up till four o'clock in the morning with other people's husbands? You are the only woman who does this kind of thing.'

And then he presented me with statements they claimed to have extracted from these men: alleged meetings with five or six of them in Nelson's bedroom.

Those were horrible days. I hate to recall them. and I was already quite sick when I went to prison. I hadn't been able to sleep at all and in prison it was the same; sometimes I wasn't able to sleep for twenty-four hours. To have something to do, I started scraping off the paint from the wall with my fingernails and at one stage I found underneath the paint an inscription which I could read quite clearly: 'Mrs Mandela is a sell-out.'

And then Swanepoel asked me, 'What do you think you are resisting? You are politically naked.' He said that I was stripped of every friend in the struggle. 'We have succeeded in telling people that you want to work for us, it hardly makes a difference to us whether you want to work for us or not. Do you want to work for us, so that we release you from prison?'

I would have come out in the very first month of those seventeen months in solitary confinement if I had agreed to the ludicrous suggestions that were made: that if I co-operated and allowed my voice to be used over the air to call upon our ANC forces at the border to retreat and put down their arms and have discussions with the government, I would be released. I was actually going to be flown by helicopter to see Nelson—with top-ranking police officers—to hold secret discussions with Nelson on the island, and after that he would be removed from the other prisoners and put into the cottage where the late Robert Sobukwe was held on the island. My husband would suffer more comfortably. They never gave up—right through my detention. That's how narrow-minded these people can be. After you've given the best years of your life to this cause—that they can dream that your principles can still be for sale! If there weren't people in this country who would still fight for justice, my fate would have been the same as that of most blacks in this land. Most blacks in this country go to jail for nothing: thousands are arrested every day whose only offence is wanting to live together as a family. I was lucky to have lawyers for my defence who have done everything to prove my innocence in court.

I forgot to say I had the Bible, because it was such a meaningless document in those circumstances. I read it four times. I never knew it was possible to read the Bible from beginning to end.

What was so ironical—we know how religious Afrikaners want to appear. Well, the way I got the Bible in prison—one of the Security men stood at the entrance, the door was flung open and he threw the Bible at my feet—'There is the Bible, ask your God to release your from jail!'

Even for people who are not very religious, the Bible still inspires some form of respect. Now here are people who are supposed to be religious mocking this same God who they believe predestined them to be the rulers of this country. When they oppress us, they oppress us in God's name, they call themselves God's chosen people. In the name of *that* God he flung that Bible at me, and yet he stands in the pulpit every Sunday to preach what he has never believed in. The Security Police are a special breed. In order to belong you have to have this particular hatred of the black man. Otherwise how would you torture people to death for ideological differences, how would you point a machine gun at a seven-year-old child and blast his brains out? You have to be of a special breed, one I know well, which has made my life impossible. And they are the people who have taught me to hate.

I'm not saying every Afrikaner is like that; I'm saying the Afrikaner who oppresses my people is like that. They are petrified of the blackman, so much so that they actually become prisoners themselves. Look at those wardresses in prison: they are really worse prisoners than us, wearing that sordid uniform and standing for hours over us—what type of person goes for that job? And once you try to communicate with them through English, they see red. These girls don't know a word in English, not even a greeting. And which political prisoner would speak Afrikaans in prison! So there is just no level of communication, only a total breakdown.

They didn't let black warders come near us—we had only white warders and wardresses.

When they brought our food in the morning, it was porridge. That was how we knew it was morning. They would take the sanitary buckets and bring them back without even rinsing them, turn the lid upside down, and put the plate of food on that lid.

It was impossible to eat. They used to put the plates of food outside next to the cells and by the time it came, it was full of bird shit—besides the porridge was uncooked.

We didn't get the same food as Coloured prisoners and the Indians. They get coffee, tea, bread and sugar. 'Bantu' [Blacks] get porridge without sugar, and something pitch black with lumps in it supposed to be coffee.

Lunch was supposed to be better, but the spinach and carrots were just as they were from the garden, unwashed, impossible to swallow. For supper we had porridge again which often floated in blood. They must have cooked meat in the pot. So we went on a hunger strike for a week, although it was difficult to communicate. We did it by banging on the wall.

We tried to raise complaints with the doctors but they would just rush through, looking briefly inside, shouting '*Klagte?*' ['Any complaints?'], and by the time you are supposed to reply, he is already ten paces away.

I suffered from malnutrition; the complexion becomes sallow, you get bleeding gums from lack of vitamins; I could not stand, I had fever and blackouts. When we were to be charged in October, I could not appear in court. I had to be taken to the prison hospital.

The only time we had some relief was when our complaints were raised in court by our lawyers. George Bizos had to apply to court for us to have baths—up to that date we hadn't been showering or washing.

There was no improvement in the prison food as a result of the hunger strike, but at least we got our food from relatives. They never stopped trying to humiliate us. When we prepared for the court case, my family brought me some clothes. When we came back to our cells after consulting with our attorneys, not only had they emptied the suitcase on the floor but they had opened jars of cosmetics and thrown them on the clothes. There was cream all over and muddy footprints. I had no way of washing or ironing them! I stood there at the door—then came the stripping, the usual process—and when I saw the woman in charge of the prison, I was so angry I saw red, the same as I had when that policeman came to my bedroom. I don't know how she escaped that cell. No human being can go on taking those humiliations without reaction.

I got more liberated in prison. The physical identification with your beliefs is far more satisfying than articulating them on a platform. My soul has been more purified by prison than anything else. I am not saying it is best to be in prison. But under the circumstances, where it is a question of which prison is better, the prison outside or inside—the whole country is a prison for the black man—and when you are inside, you know why you are there, and the people who put you there also know.

Follow On

The Moses of Her People

Before Reading

'The Moses of Her People' is made up of a series of short extracts from a full length biography of Harriet Tubman by Anne Petry called *'Harriet Tubman: Conductor on the Underground Railway'* (Pocket Books). Anne Petry wrote this book because she believes 'that the majority of textbooks used in schools do not give an adequate or accurate picture of the history of slavery in the United States'.

● Discuss what you already know about the fight against slavery between 1830–1866 and note down the names of some of the people involved. The titles in 'Further Reading' will provide you with some of the information you need.

During Reading

● Make a note of any points you would like more information about. These could be used later as research into this period of history.

● Look out for details of how the network of people who made up the Underground Railway worked together to bring about the escapes.

After Reading

● 'It was as the storyteller, the bard, that Harriet's active years came to a close.'
    From the information you have gathered about Harriet Tubman and the Underground Railway, and using your own imagination, write a story about an escape during this time.

● Using the booklist provided in 'Further Reading', conduct your own piece of research into one area of this period of history.

● Find out more about some of the people who actively opposed slavery but who are all too often left out of school text books. For example:

    Olandah Eguiano, David Walker, Nat Turner, Sojourner Truth, Ida B. Wells, Fredrick Douglas and Mary Church Terrell.

● Make an extended study of fiction and autobiographies which cover this period.

● Draw up a proposal for a television programme about Harriet Tubman. In pairs decide what form you would like this programme to take. For example:

A drama about part of Harriet Tubman's life, perhaps focusing on one of the escapes she helped to organise.

A drama–documentary about her life, using material you could research about this period of history, and short dramatisations of parts of her life.

A documentary based around a research project done by school students in which they describe what they have found out about her and how they did it.

Write a description outlining your proposal, including the audience the programme would be aimed at and how long it will last.

A Belfast Woman

Before Reading

This story was taken from an anthology of short stories by Mary Becket entitled 'A Belfast Woman' (Poolbeg Press Ltd). All her stories focus on the domestic, social and political tension rife in Northern Ireland during the past half centrury. 'A Belfast Woman' has been called a definitive Belfast *Mother Courage*.

● In order to get the most from this story you need to find out about the history of Ireland.

Think about the following questions:

1 When and why did the present 'Troubles' in the North of Ireland begin?

2 Why were the houses of Catholic families being burnt out in 1921 and 1972?

3 In 1935 why did Catholic families receive letters threatening that their houses would be burnt down unless they moved out? Why did Protestant families receive similar letters in the 1970s?

4 Why is it dangerous for Catholics to go and live in 'Protestant Streets', and for Catholics and Protestants to set up in business together?

5 Who are 'Fenians' and 'Tacques'? Why would some people use these words as insults and others be proud of them?

6 Why would Mary, the central character of this story, have believed in the 1950s that 'clever poor Catholics' couldn't get better jobs than working as a teacher or in the Post Office?

7   Why are the areas of the Ardoyne and the Divis flats so well known?

If you want to find out more about the history of Ireland, the titles in 'Further Reading' will provide you with some of the information you need.

During Reading

● 'A Belfast Woman' is written as a first person narrative, with the narrator recounting some of the main events in her life from 1921 until the present day. Notice how the story moves between the present (where it begins and ends) and the past. Either during or after reading, note down the major events or episodes in the narrator's life, what she felt about them, and any dates that will help place them in chronological order. For example:

EVENT/EPISODE	NARRATOR'S FEELING/REACTION	DATE
Parents' home burnt out	Terrified – 'wasn't able to sleep for weeks'	1921

After Reading

● Mary is a very strong woman. Write a character study of Mary showing how she dealt with the adversities in her life and how she still managed to have hope by the end of the story. Include what you thought gave her this strength, and the impression you got of her through the way she told her story.

● You have been given an assignment to report on the situation in Belfast for TV news. You have been given five minutes air time in which to interview and comment upon present day life in Belfast. Using the information you have researched, and Mary as your interviewee, write a script for this television news report.

● Some of you may have lived in situations that are volatile and frightening. Drawing on your own experiences, feelings, worries and hopes, write a poem or a piece of prose that conveys the trauma of this situation.

● Write a story that uses conflict as the background whilst centring on the experience of one or two people involved in it.

My Army Life

Before Reading

This extract is taken from *'Hsieh Ping-Ying: Autobiography of a Chinese Girl'*, translated into English by Tsui Chi (Pandora Press). The autobiography covers the first thirty years of her life.

Hsieh Ping-Ying was born in either 1903 or 1906 (sources vary). She grew up at a time of great social and economic change. The once powerful Middle Kingdom had been fragmented and was being fought over by warlords and foreign powers. Traditional Chinese philosophies and customs were being questioned and overturned. The ideal of romantic love was being set against arranged marriages, agility and mobility were set against footbinding, and seclusion and new forms of female education and occupation were set against domestic services and dependence in marriage.

The Student Movement of 4 May began in Peking (now Beijing). Its aims were to discredit the old customs, beliefs and institutions, and to introduce new western values of individualism, equality and democracy. Young people passionately wanted to unify China and throw out the foreign powers which took over parts of their country after the First World War.

In 1926 a march from Canton to the central valley of the Yangtze River began. This was called the Northern Expedition. One of its aims was to bring the new ideas to the peasants through a well planned programme of education and propaganda. In order to achieve this a number of schools were set up to recruit, and train young female students to join the army. Hsieh Ping-Ying was enrolled at The Wuchang Central Political and Military School. She was one of twenty girl propagandists selected to travel with the army on its first expedition into the Hanon province.

During Reading

● When Hsieh Ping-Ying learnt that her army was to be demobilised she thought 'Tomorrow was the time when we should go into hell.' Look out for examples from the extract which support this feeling.

● Look for examples of style and vocabulary which could indicate that this extract is a translation.

After Reading

● In later years Hsieh Ping-Ying earnt her living by writing stories based on her own experiences. Using this extract as a starting point, write an imaginative story about what happened to Shu Yun after demobilisation.

● Use the titles in further reading to find out more about the changing role of girls and women in China during this century.

Muriel

Before Reading

This extract first appeared in *'Images of Ourselves: Women with disabilities talking'*, edited by Jo Campling (Routledge and Kegan Paul).

Jo Campling is able-bodied but she was brought up in a 'disabled family' since her mother had had polio at the age of three. Jo began work on *'Images of Ourselves'* after completing a handbook for people with disabilities called *'Better Lives for Disabled Women'* (Virago). In her introduction to *'Images of Ourselves'* she writes:

'I asked my friends to write whatever they wanted about their situations as women with disabilities. I rejected the idea of interviews because even the most skilled interviewer cannot help but be directive. I did not want the impromptu answer but deeply felt, considered contibution.'

During Reading

● Look out for the things which Muriel has strong feelings about, in particular the way she feels able–bodied people misunderstand disabled people.

After Reading

● In pairs re–read the extract and make notes on:
    The biographical details we learn about Muriel's life;
    The issues she feels strongly about in relation to disabled people.
Join up with another one or two pairs and compare your notes. Also discuss what you have learned about the needs of disabled people as a result of reading the extract. For example:
    Did what Muriel had to say make you revise any opinions you previously had?
    Did anything surprise you?
    Did you agree with all the points she made?
Using your notes and the points raised by your discussion complete one of the following assignments:

● Write a review of this extract, or the whole book if you can get hold of a copy, for a magazine read by young people in which you say what impact it made on you, what you learnt from it and how it changed your opinions.

● In small groups plan a ten minute reading of sections of this extract for the rest of the class, in which you give details of Muriel's life and show her beliefs and attitudes. Prepare and rehearse your reading and then perform it.

● Carry out your own research into an aspect of disablement. Your local library and the following organisation will provide you with some of the information you need: Disabled Advise Service, Atheldene Community Centre, Garratt Lane, London SW18. (01-870-7437).

● Local Education Authorities all have policies for educating people with disabilities. You can find out what the policy is for your area, and what facilities there are for disabled school students, by contacting your LEA office. Based on the information you collect, write up your findings in the form of an article for the local paper.

● Conduct a survey at your school into the adaptations and changes that would have to be made to make it fully accessible for people who have to use wheelchairs.

A Jury of Her Peers

Before Reading

This story was first published in 1917, when women were not allowed to sit on juries. Susan Glaspell (1882–1948) grew up in Iowa and the events of this story were suggested to her when she was working for an American newspaper. A half hour video of the story is available from the ILEA film and video library (for ILEA teachers only) or *The Cinema of Women*, 27 Clerkenwell Close, London EC1 (01-251-4978).

● The title of this story suggests that a woman is to be tried for committing a crime.
In pairs, find in the story the following *PAIRS* of extracts and discuss what they suggest to you. For example:
What clues do they give you about what has happened?
Do they represent similar or differing points of view?
Do they complement or contradict one another?
After you have finished reading and discussing the extracts, prepare a short statement which says what you think happened. Also give your opinion as to why some of the extracts were paired.

1a   From 'When Martha Hale opened the storm door' to 'half the flour sifted and half unsifted.' (44)

b   From 'She looked around the kitchen' to 'unfinished things always bothered her.' (53)

2a   From '"You're convinced there was nothing"' to 'the insignificance of kitchen things.' (50)

b   From '"the law is the law"' to 'never going over to see Minnie Foster—.' (56)

3a   From 'Mrs Peters' husband broke into a laugh' to 'used to worrying over trifles.' (51)

b   From 'Mrs Hale, still leaning against the door' to 'makes things harder for Minnie Foster.' (46)

4a   From 'They were so engaged' to '"out in the barn and get that cleared up."' (57)

b   From '"The sewing" said Mrs Peters' to 'pulled a knot and drawn the threads.' (57)

5a   From '"Well, that's very interesting"' to '"superstitious you know, they leave."' (62)

b   From '"Somebody wrung its neck"' to '"choked the life out of him."' (61)

6a   From '"No, Peters" said the county attorney' to '"clumsy way of doing it."' (64)

b   From '"Oh, I wish I'd come over"' to '"what we know this minute?"' (63)

7a   From '"No; Mrs Peters doesn't need supervising"' to 'chuckled Mrs Peters' husband.' (65)

b   From 'For a moment Mrs Peters did not move' to 'county attorney came back into the kitchen.' (66)

During Reading

● Look out for examples which show the attitudes the men have towards the women, and the women have towards the men. Also, look out for the clues found by the women and those found by the men which indicate a crime has been committed.

● This story was written early in the twentieth century and is set in Dickson County in America. Find examples in the style of writing which help to indicate the period and the place. An obvious example is the way the author names her characters, both in description and in dialogue. Notice that she sometimes breaks conventions and refers to 'Mrs Hale's husband' instead of calling him Mr Hale; she also makes a point of refering to Minnie by her first and unmarried name. Why do you think she made these decisions?

After Reading

● In pairs discuss what you consider her aim was in writing this story, and why you think she chose to call it 'A Jury of Her Peers'. As part of your discussion consider the following questions:

1 Why did she choose to write this story as a third person narrative rather than a first person narrative?
2 Who do you consider to be the central character in the story and why?
3 A number of 'crimes' are uncovered during the story. What are they?
4 Why has the author included so many references to women being concerned with 'trifles' rather than 'important' things?
5 Why has she chosen to include details of each woman's past in the story?
6 Throughout the story Martha Hale is worried by 'things half done'. Do you consider this to be an important theme within the story?

● Write the story of what takes place when Mrs Peters visits Mrs Wright in prison to deliver her things.

● Write the story of what takes place when Martha Hale decides to visit.

● Write or act out parts of the scene from the trial of Mrs Wright.

Smoke

Before Reading

'Smoke' was originally written in Gujarati, and was translated into English by Sima Sharma. Ila Arab Mehta is a professor of Gujarati at St Xaviers College, Bombay, and has won awards for her writing. She has also written for radio and television.

'Smoke' was first published in *'Truth Tales: Stories by Indian Women'* edited by Kali for Women. Kali is the Hindu goddess of power, the female counterpart of Shiva, the god of destruction.

● With a friend consider some of the secrets that we may have to keep from those around us, especially our families. Some may be minor, others could cause considerable upset if they were discovered. Also consider what kinds of secrets the adults in your family may wish to keep. Of course you do not have to give any of these away, but it may be interesting to suggest some secrets you think are commonly kept by young people and by adults, and to share them with the rest of the class.

During Reading

● Stop reading at the end of the paragraph beginning 'Home at last,' and discuss:
   The relationship between Shubha, Ba, Subadh and Bapuji;
   The way the author presents the relationship between Shubha and Ba in the opening pages of the story;
   If you think Shubha will be successful in keeping her smoking a secret from Ba.

● Consider the narrative style and structure of the story.
For example:
   Why has the author chosen a third person narrative?
   From whose point of view do we see events?
   If you were to divide the story into two or more sections, where would you put the breaks?
   In general, how would you describe the language of the story? Formal/descriptive/colloquial/poetic/conversational? Look for examples to back up your choice.

After Reading

● A reviewer of 'Smoke' wrote:
   'Although the author has chosen to hang her story around Shubha's secret addiction to smoking, it is only a symptom of the general situation she is exploring in the story. Giving up smoking would not immediately change Shubha's life.'

In pairs or small groups discuss this point of view. As part of your discussion you may find it useful to consider the meaning of the following quotations within the story as a whole. (Before discussing each quotation re-read the paragraphs either side of it.)
   1   From 'A crystal bowl decked', to 'one by one to be put away'. (p.69)
   2   From 'That is how it should be – some give and take,' to 'two dimensional stills'. (p.70)
   3   From 'Beneath the words', to 'I know it all … everything.' (p.72)
   4   From 'She had lingered too long', to 'afraid to come alive.' (p.72)

● Imagine that Shubha and Ba both keep a diary. Write an entry for each on the night the story ends.

● Continue the story from where it ends. As far as possible write in the style of the original. After you have finished each of you could read your 'endings' to the rest of the class.

● Write a story of your own in which you explore some of the themes and issues within the story.

The Picture

Before Reading

This story was translated into English by Denys Johnson-Davies. Latifa el-Zayat is well known in Egypt for her novel 'The Open Door', her short stories, and her book reviews and commentary in Cairo newspapers. In the autumn of 1981 she was arrested in a general crack-down of intellectuals with controversial views. She was imprisoned for two months with a group which included the physician and feminist writer Nawal el Saadawi.

● Choose two or three photographs from your family album which conjure up specific memories and feelings. In pairs closely examine the setting, people, expressions and movement. Try to spend ten minutes remembering all the circumstances surrounding the picture. If you were not present when the picture was taken, imagine in detail what was going through the minds of the people in the picture.

During Reading

● Look out for the clues the author gives which show:
  That the marriage held worries for Amal;
  Izzat's attitude towards his marriage.

● Carefully re–read the section where the photograph is taken, from 'Amal remained standing, watching the two of them..'. (p.80) to the end of the story. Note Amal's reasons for wanting it to be taken and her reasons for tearing it up.

After Reading

● At first, Amal sees the white woman as a temptress, but later she

recognises her disappointment in her husband's behaviour.
Do you think the white woman was suitably behaved? Argue your
case giving examples from the text. Look for examples which illus-
trate the way she presents herself, and what she actually does with
the family.

● We feel great sympathy for Amal because of her realisation about,
and disappointment in, her husband. Show in detail with examples
from the text, how the author manages to make us feel sympathy for
Amal.

● The last line of the story is 'Amal realised she had a long way to
go.' Write a story about Amal set ten years later.

● Create your own story where a picture is vital to the plot.

● Write short but detailed descriptions of a series of old photographs as though you were looking through a photo album. They
may be linked in some way or they may be separate. Whichever you
choose, your descriptions must evoke the atmosphere and style of
the photograph as well as the setting and the people.

   You may like to write a series of poems instead of prose descriptions.

Caroline's Piece

Before Reading

The word 'Holocaust' means the purposeful destruction and annihi-
lation of a whole group of people. During the Second World War, the
Nazi Party systematically tried to destroy and annihilate the Jewish
people, and they succeeded in murdering six million Jews. Some
tried to escape this persecution and became refugees. Caroline is the
daughter of Jewish refugees from Germany. Her complete chapter,
and three more written by other daughters of Jewish refugees can be
found in *'You'd Prefer Me Not To Mention It: The lives of four Jewish
daughters of refugees'*, (Calvert's North Star Press).

   These women met and formed a group specifically to address certain questions that had been left out of their education at home, at
schools and in society generally. Caroline wanted to know why her
family had been forced to flee the country of their birth, why her
parents had been persecuted, what effect that had had on her family
life and what it meant for her future. In addition Caroline wanted to
write about the process she went through in discovering and
reclaiming a positive Jewish identity.

To understand this extract you need to have some background knowledge of what happened in Europe between 1930–47. The titles in 'Further Reading' will give you some of the information you need.

● Working with another person, try and list some ideas and reasons why you think it is important for people to communicate to others about their parents' or their own lives.

During Reading

● In 'Letter to my mother' look out for references to:
The historical events;
The ways in which Caroline appreciates her mother's guidance.

● Caroline asks 'What does the Holocaust mean to me?' What do you think her feelings are?

● In 'Ode to the English' look out for the words or phrases that convey Caroline's anger.

After Reading

● In small groups discuss your reactions to these extracts. Try and examine your own feelings towards the historical events Caroline writes about, and how she presents herself through them.

● There are three separate styles used here, a letter, a discussion, and a poem. In each, Caroline speaks of the way her life has been affected by the past. Write an essay about this way of presenting information. Does it tell you enough factually? Does it show the results of her type of upbringing clearly?

● Write a letter to a parent or guardian in which you tell him/her the ways in which you feel he/she has influenced your life.

● Caroline wrote this piece for the 'Jewish Women's History Group'. One of the aims of this group was to show a wider audience the ways in which history has affected them, and all of us. In what way do you feel history has affected you and your family? Try to write an essay, play or poem which conveys how your life has been affected by the past. You may wish to work with another person or a small group, to discuss and explore the subject before you write.

● Devise your own research project concerning aspects of this story. For example you could look at the immigration of Jews, or any other ethnic groups, into Britain and discover why they came and what happened to them here.

● Interview a person of your choice and through a series of searching but sensitive questions, build up a picture of that person's cultural identity.

● Devise an oral history project where you select a person or a small group of people to tell their stories in their own way. Encourage the telling of these stories, and then document, record and research around the information you have gathered. Photographs and other evidence can be used to back up your written findings. You could then make an exhibition of your work.

Dreaming the Sky Down

Before Reading

This story first appeared in an anthology of short stories by Barbara Burford called *'The Threshing Floor'*, (Sheba Feminist Publishers). Each of the stories in the anthology reflects back women's experience and strength, and the central characters span a wide age range. Some of Barbara Burford's poetry has also been published in *'A Dangerous Knowing: Four Black Women Poets'*, Barbara Burford, Gabriella Pearce, Grace Nichols and Jackie Kay (Sheba).

● Dreams can sometimes feel more real than life itself. Discuss with a partner or in a small group, your most vivid dreams. When you have exchanged a variety of dreams, try to evaluate how much you feel they were influenced by your experiences during the day.

● Dreams don't always add up or make complete sense. It's the feelings they evoke which make the pictures more vivid. Write a dream sequence that combines these vivid pictures with strong emotional reactions.

During Reading

● In the story Donna is portrayed as having very strong feelings. Look out for the incidents you feel annoy her.

● Find key words or phrases that convey Donna's freedom and exhilaration when she is flying.

After Reading

● In pairs re-read the dream sequences in the story (pages 88, 91, 93,

99). Choose one sequence each and try to sketch in words, phrases, poems, pictures or cartoons what the sequence means to you.

● Imagine that you have available all the technical equipment necessary to make whatever visual and audio special effects you wish. Script one of the sequences from the story for film or video, describing in detail any special effects you wish to include. Then devise your own dream sequence and write a similar script.

● Donna uses flying as a method of relieving her feelings of oppression, frustration and anger. Devise your own 'freedom exit' and write a story.

Caving

Mel Kathchild lives in South London with her child and works as a part-time journalist and advice worker, struggling to find more time to write stories.

Before Reading

● What does the title of this short story indicate it may be about?

● Working in pairs or small groups, tell each other about a school trip you enjoyed. Try and include the following points in your tale:

1 Where and when the trip took place
2 Who was present and a brief description of the more memorable characters
3 Any incident which was amusing or dangerous
4 What you got out of it

● Working in pairs or in small groups, plan a trip for one of the following:
An adventure day for you and your friend(s);
A day out with ten five-year olds;
An afternoon out with twenty pensioners.

During Reading

● Look out for the tactics the guide uses to make the girls take notice of him. Do you approve of his approach?

● Stop reading at the end of the paragraph beginning 'So they all got on their bellies...' (page 101) and predict what you think will happen next.

● Stop reading at the end of the paragraph beginning 'And so they walked along...' (page 108) and predict how the story will end.

After Reading

● Working in pairs within groups of 8, each pair takes on the role of one of the main characters in the story, ie. Miss, the guide, Lin, Angie. Spend some time 'preparing' your role (getting to know the character you'll be acting). Prepare some questions you think ought to be asked of your character, and questions you'd like to ask the other characters.

Take the role of your character and give the remaining seven students a chance to ask you questions, for example about the part you played in the story, why you acted in the way you did, and what you think of the other characters. Questions could include:

Why did you go on/organise a school trip like this?
Why did you become a teacher/guide?
What were you thinking when... happened?
What happened at the end of the story?

● After your discussion write one of the following:
1 A review of the story as a whole in which you discuss the author's aim in writing this story and the characters she chose to include.
2 An ending to the story in which you describe what has happened. As far as possible write in the style of the original story.
3 A report for a local newspaper about the 'accident' in which you include interviews with some of the characters involved.

● Did you suspect that this story would have a "twist" at the end? Can you trace back and discover the clues which suggested it would end in tragedy?

● Having discussed the way the author constructed her story, write one of your own with a twist at the end. Call it 'Sting In The Tail' and don't forget to lay clues along the way for your readers.

● The teacher's thoughts are given in this story so that the reader can listen to her as she goes through her day, and see her as separate from her job and how the students see her. By examining these thoughts explain what type of person you think she is.

Their Eyes Were Watching God
Before Reading

This extract is taken from a novel written by Zora Neale Hurston in

1937 called *'Their Eyes Were Watching God'* (Virago). The extract begins when Janie and Tea Cake have moved to Palm Beach, Florida, in search of work which they find as seasonal pickers in the Everglades nearby. Their work and their lives are hard, but their world is suddenly uprooted when...

During Reading

● 'Their Eyes Were Watching God' is written in unusual, almost poetic language. While you are reading look out for examples of words, phrases or sentences which:

Reveal an insight into a hidden feeling;

Show a way of being, living, or doing.

● You will also notice, that this extract has a rhythm and flow to it. It is skillfully shaped around the tempo of the hurricane. Try to find examples of words, phrases and sentences which reflect the progress of the hurricane. For example, those which convey:

The quietness before the storm:'Morning came without motion; The winds, to the tiniest, lisping baby breath had left the earth;'

The growing wildness;

The devastation.

After Reading

● In pairs re-read the extract and using the categories above collect examples of the way in which Zora Neale Hurston mirrors the pace of the hurricane in the style of her writing. Use your notes to write an essay in which you discuss the style this extract is written in.

● Jane and Teacake are strong and likeable characters. Giving examples from the story, describe these two characters by examining what they say and do, and how they live.

● There are very many different ways of speaking English. In the dialect Zora Neale Hurston uses, phrases and words convey far more than their obvious meaning. Underneath many of these phrases are other images for you to understand and conjure with.

Find about six phrases and explain what they suggest to you.

Write a poem, song or dialogue in dialect, using the idea of different layers of meaning.

Like many black writers, Zora Neale Hurston did not receive the recognition she deserved during her life time and died in relative obscurity. Since then her work as a writer, folklorist and commentator has become an inspiration to many contempary writers.

In 1973 Alice Walker made a pilgrimage to Zora Neale Hurston's birthplace in Eatonsville, Florida, in an attempt to discover more about her life and if possible discover her grave. The following is taken from *'Looking For Zora'* an account of her expedition which appears in *'In Search of Our Mother's Gardens'* (The Women's Press).

'How're you going to find anything out here?' she asks. And I stand still a few seconds, looking at the weeds. Some of them are quite pretty, with tiny yellow flowers. They are thick and healthy, but dead weeds under them have formed a thick gray carpet on the ground. A snake could be lying six inches from my big toe and I wouldn't see it. We move slowly, very slowly, our eyes alert, our legs trembly. It is hard to tell where the center of the circle is since the circle is not really round, but more like half of something round. There are things crackling and hissing in the grass. Sandspurs are sticking to the inside of my skirt. Sand and ants cover my feet. I look toward the road and notice that there are, indeed, *two* large curving stones, making an entrance and exit to the cemetery.

'Zora' I call again. 'I'm here. Are you?'

'If she is,' grumbles Rosalee, 'I hope she'll keep it to herself.'

'Zora!' Then I start fussing with her. 'I hope you don't think I'm going to stand out here all day, with these snakes watching me and these ants having a field day. In fact, I'm going to call you just one or two more times.' On a clump of dried grass, near a small bushy tree, my eye falls on one of the largest bugs I have ever seen. It is on its back, and is as large as three of my fingers. I walk toward it, and yell 'Zo-ra!' and my foot sinks into a hole. I look down. I am standing in a sunken rectangle that is about six feet long and about three or four feet wide. I look up to see where the two gates are.

'Well,' I say, 'this is the center, or approximately anyhow. It's also the only sunken spot we've found. Doesn't this look like a grave to you?'...

There are times—and finding Zora Hurston's grave was one of them—when normal responses of grief, horror, and so on do not make sense because they bear no real relation to the depth of the emotion one feels. It was impossible for me to cry when I saw the field full of weeds where Zora is. Partly this is because I have come to know Zora through her books and she was not a teary sort of person herself; but partly, too, it is because there is a point at which even grief feels absurd. And at this point, laughter gushes up to retrieve sanity.

If you wish to find out more about her life and work, the titles in 'Further Reading' will help you.

The Little School

Before Reading

This extract is from' *The Little School Tales of Disappearance and Survival in Argentina'*(Virago). Alicia Partnoy was born in 1955 in Argentina. Because of her opposition to the military dictatorship, she was "detained" on 12 January 1977 and taken to a concentration camp called, ironically, 'The Little School.' So she became one of the 30,000 who "disappeared" between 1976 and 1979. In her introduction to her book she writes:

> On 25 April after three and a half months, the guards told me they were taking me "to see how the radishes grow" – a euphemism for death and burial. Instead I was transferred from the Little School to another place where I remained "disappeared" for fifty-two more days... I "reappeared" but remained a political prisoner for two and a half more years.

In her book she speaks through the voices of some of the women she met inside The Little School, as well as her own and that of a third person narrator. For example, in the parts of this extract entitled 'Graciela: Around the Table' and 'Nativity', Graciela becomes the narrator.

● Imagine you have "disappeared"—forcibly removed from family and friends. You are able to smuggle out one letter. What would you write? Who would you write to? Would you ask for help or for someone to take care of your affairs? Try and write this letter, remembering it's the only one you know will reach the outside world.

During Reading

Look out for the following phrases and assess why they meant so much to the women in the chapter.

> 'It felt nice to be wearing a loose house dress and her slippers after having slept so many nights with her shoes on, waiting for them.' (p.120)
> '... she discovered a ragged blanket. She used it to cover her feet and did not feel so helpless.' (p.121)
> '... we gave up sunshine on our skin for your future.' (p.124)
> 'The first four cans were making the sweetest music she had heard in a very long time.' (p.124)
> 'I own a leak.' (p.125)
> 'A story that made her laugh just because she was not allowed to laugh.' (p.127)

● There are many ways in which the guards try to break their prisoners' spirits. As you read look out for what they are and how the prisoners respond to them.

After Reading

● At the end of her book Alicia Partnoy includes an appendix in which she describes what happened to the women who "disappeared" with her. This is what happened to Graciela and María Elena.

The case of Graciela Alicia Romero de Metz

Graciela was arrested on 16 December 1976 in Cutral Co (Neuquén) along with her husband, Raul Eugenio Metz. Heavily armed individuals broke into their home, also threatening the neighbours. Both were 24 years old at the time of their detention. They had one daughter, Adrianita, who was two or three years old; once detained, they received no news of her fate. Graciela was five months pregnant at the time, and during the transfer by truck to Neuquén she was tortured with electric shocks to her stomach and hit brutally.

Later they were both transferred to the Little School. Raul was forced to remain prone on the floor, hands tied behind his back. Towards the end of January he was taken, according to the guards, to Neuquén. A writ of habeas corpus was requested. His name is registered in Amnesty International's list of disappeared people.

Graciela stayed at the Little School, forced to remain prone, blindfolded and handcuffed like the rest. In the last month of her pregnancy she was permitted "exercise"—blindfolded walks around a table, holding on to the edge. A few days before giving birth they took her to a trailer on the patio. On 17 April she had a son—normally, but without medical assistance. Other prisoners persistently asked the guards to let them help her or keep her company, but they didn't allow it. She was helped by the guards. On 23 April she was removed from the Little School and never heard of again. She is on Amnesty International's list of disappeared people. Her son, according to the guards, was given to one of the interrogators.

The case of María Elena Romero

María Elena was arrested on 6 February 1977 at her home by plainclothesmen who were heavily armed. She was 17 years old. María Elena was Graciela Romero's sister. María Elena was taken from the Little School the night of 12 April and shot.

● In all these extracts the women show great courage in keeping up their resistance. Draw a diagram with the prisoners in the middle and on the outside write down some of the different ways in which they were tortured. In between the two, write down what the women did and thought to block these assaults.

Using this diagram write an essay entitled 'Resistance In The Little School'.

● It is some time later and you have been commissioned by a television station to make a documentary about what happened in The Little School. You are able to interview guards as well as prisoners.

Write out a section of this documentary. A plan such as this one may help:

CAMERA SHOTS	INTERVIEWER	INTERVIEWEE
1) Long view of The Little School and surrounding area	*Question 1*: When did you arrive at the Little School?	*Answer 1*: It must have been late at night in January.

Winnie Mandela: Detention and Trial 1969

Before Reading

In the Editorial Note to *Winnie Mandela: Part of my Soul* (Penguin Books Ltd) which this extract is taken from, Anne Benjamin explains how the book was put together:

> This is not an autobiography in the conventional sense. The restrictions placed on her activities by the government and her daily involvement in the liberation movement make it impossible for Winnie Mandela to sit down and write a book. This book was compiled outside South Africa, and although Mrs Mandela was fully informed about the project, she could not see the manuscript in detail before it went into print.

● In pairs or small groups discuss what you already know about Winnie Mandela and the struggle against apartheid in South Africa (Anzania). Note down the points raised in your discussion and share them with the rest of the class.

● Find out more about the system of apartheid enforced in South Africa. The titles in 'Further Reading' will provide you with some of the information you need.

During Reading

● Early on in this extract Winnie Mandela says of her detention 'The whole thing was calculated to destroy you, not only morally but also physically'. Look out for examples of the tactics used by the authorities to break down her will, and the ways in which she managed to resist them.

After Reading

● Look at the list of charges and court cases brought against Winnie Mandela since her detention in 1969.

1970   Banning order renewed for five years, plus house arrest each night and during weekends—visitors forbidden.

1970   Accused of violating her banning order by receiving visitors—five relations (two of them children) who called at her house.
Sentence: Six months' imprisonment suspended for three years, this was set aside on appeal.

1971   Accused of violating her banning order: communication with a banned person in her house (Peter Magubane). Sentence: Twelve months' imprisonment suspended for three years. Conviction and sentence were set aside on appeal.

1973   Accused of violating her banning order: lunch with her children in a Combi in the presence of a banned person (Peter Magubane). Sentence: Twelve months' imprisonment suspended for three years.

1974   On appeal in October 1974 sentence was reduced to six months, which she served in Kroonstad Prison.

1975   Third banning order expired; ten months' 'freedom' (after thirteen years of banning).

1976   Detained in 12 August under Section 6 of the Internal Security Act after Soweto uprising; imprisoned in the 'Fort' in Johannesburg until December 1976.

1977   Banning order renewed for five years.

1977   Banished to Brandfort in the Orange Free State on 17 May.

1977   Countless arrests in Brandfort because of violations of her banning
–9   order, almost daily, sometimes twice daily. She refuses to keep 'such a despicable statistic.'

1978   Court case on alleged incitement of the Soweto uprising; acquitted and awarded compensation for defamation.

1980   Accused of assaulting a policeman while in Johannesburg; found not guilty and acquitted.

1980   Accused of violating her banning order by having a friend of the family as a lodger in her house in Brandfort; case postponed.

1982   Banning order renewed for another five years.

1982   Numerous charges in connection with violations of her banning
–5   order, but few were brought to court.

● Using your own knowledge, or by further reading, carry out your own research into an aspect of the struggle against the apartheid regime in South Africa. For example, you could complete one of the following assignments:

1)   Bring the chronology of charges and court cases against Winnie Mandela up to date.

2)   Find out what is involved in a 'banning order'. (An example of the banning order served on Winnie Mandela in 1976 is given on pages 157–160 of '*Part of My Soul*'.)

Further Reading

The Moses of Her People
The People Who Came Book 3, E Braithwaite and A Phillips, Longman Caribbean; *A Breath of Fresh Air*, G Kaye, Adlib Paperbacks; Write to NATE, Birley School Annexe, Fox Lane Site, Frecheville, Sheffield, S12 4WY for a comprehensive book list.

A Belfast Woman
Lifting the Lid, U Barry, Attic Press; *Only the Rivers Run Free*, E Fairweather *et al*, Pluto Press; *In the Eyes of the Law*, N McCafferty, Poolbeg Press; *Holy Island*, N Hoult, Arlen House; *Mary Lavelle*, K O' Brien, Virago; *Selected Plays – Irish Drama Selections 3*, C Smythe and M Fitzgerald (eds) CUA Press.

My Army Life
The Dragon's Village, Yuan-Tsung Chen, The Women's Press; *Leaden Wings*, Jie Zhang, Virago; *As Long as Nothing Happens, Nothing Will*, Jie Zhang, Virago.

Muriel
What it's like to be me (by disabled children) H Exley (ed), Exley; *Skipper*, K Marchant, Hodder & Stoughton; *With Wings: An anthology of literature by and about Women with Disabilities*, M Saxton and F Howe (eds), The Feminist Press; *Cushla and Her Books*, D Butler, Penguin; *Living Outside Inside*, S Hannaford, Canterbury Press.

Jury of Her Peers
Portraits, K Chopin, The Women's Press; *The Charlotte Perkins Gilman Reader*, The Women's Press; *Brown Girl, Brown Stones*, P Marshall, Virago; *The Experience of the American Woman*, H Soloman (ed) Mentor.

Smoke
Right of Way, Asian Women's Writers Workshop, The Women's Press; *The Scarlet Thread: An Indian Woman Speaks*, R Barton (ed), Virago; *Sumitra's Story*, R Smith, M Books.

Caroline's Piece
The Holocaust Denial, G Seidel, 'Beyond the Pale' Collective; *Nice Jewish Girls: A Lesbian Anthology*, T Beck (ed), The Crossing Press; *Bread Givers*, A Yezierska, The Women's Press; *Tribe of Dina*, M Kay *et al*, Sinister Wisdom Books; *The Jewish East End Education Pack*; L Hart *et al*, Tower Hamlets Environment Trust.

The Picture
Khul-Khaal: Five Egyptian Women Tell Their Stories, N Atiya, Virago; *Memoirs from the Women's Prison*, Nawal el Sa'adawi, The Women's Press; *Both Right and Left Handed*, Bouthaina Shaabau, The Women's Press; *My Life Story*, Fadhamar Amrouche, The Women's Press.

Dreaming the Sky Down
Watchers and Seekers, R Cobham and M Collins (eds), The Women's Press; *The Heart of the Race*, B Bryan *et al*, Virago.

Caving
The Women of Brewster Place, G Naylor, Sphere Books; *Breaking Training*, S Welch, Fontana Lions; *Annie on My Mind*, N Garden, Virago Upstarts; *True to Life*, S Hemmings (ed), Sheba; *Girls are Powerful*, S Hemmings, Sheba.

Their Eyes Were Watching God
Dust Tracks on a Road, Z N Hurston, Virago; *Spunk!*, Z N Hurston, Camden Press; *In Search of Our Mother's Gardens*, A Walker, The Women's Press; *Zora Neale Hurston: A Literary Biography*, R E Hemenway, Camden Press.
The Little School
Women's Resistance: Poetry from Latin America, A Hopkins (ed), The Women's Press; *They Won't Take Me Alive*, C Alegria, The Women's Press; *Talking in Whispers*, J Watson, Fontana.
Detention and Trial
The Child is not Dead: Youth Resistance in South Africa, A Harris *et al*, ILEA Learning Resources Branch; *The Apartheid Handbook*, R Ormond, Penguin; *Call me Woman*, E Kuzwayo, The Women's Press; *South Africa: The Cordoned Heart* (Essays by Twenty South African Photographers), O Badshar (ed), W W Norton; *We Make Freedom: Women in South Africa*, B Lipman (ed) Pandora.

Acknowledgements

The editors and publisher thank the following for permission to reproduce the material in this collection:

'The Moses of Her People' © Anne Petry, from *Harriet Tubman: Conductor on the Underground Railway*, Thomas Y Crowell, USA
'A Belfast Woman' © Mary Becket, Poolbeg Press Ltd, 1980
'Demobilisation' from *My Army Life* by Hsieh-Ping-Ying, Pandora
'Muriel' from *Images of Ourselves* edited by Jo Campling, Routledge & Kegan Paul
'Smoke' © Ila Arab Mehta from *Truth Tales*, edited by Kali for Women, The Women's Press
'Caroline's Piece' from *You'd Prefer Me Not To Mention It* originally published by Calvert's North Star Press
'Dreaming the Sky Down' © Barbara Burford, originally published in *The Threshing Floor* by Barbara Burford, Sheba Feminist Publishers, 1986
'Caving' © Mel Kathchild
Extract from *Their Eyes Were Watching God* by Zora Neale Hurston, originally published by Virago
Extracts from *The Little School* by Alicia Partnoy, originally published by Virago
'Detention and Trial' by Winnie Mandela, edited by Anne Benjamin © Rowohlt Taschenbech Verlag GmbH, 1984, reproduced by permission of Penguin Books Ltd, 1985

While every attempt has been made to contact the copyright holders, this has not proved possible in every case. We would be pleased to hear from anyone not credited.